TABLE OF CONTENTS

Top 20 Test Taking Tips 5

Pharmacology of Addictive Substances 6

Theoretical Base of Counseling 26

Counseling Practice 34

Professional Issues 59

Practice Test 68

    Practice Questions 68

    Answer Explanations 82

Secret Key #1 - Time is Your Greatest Enemy 91

    Pace Yourself 91

Secret Key #2 - Guessing is not Guesswork 91

    Monkeys Take the Test 91

    $5 Challenge 92

Secret Key #3 - Practice Smarter, Not Harder 93

    Success Strategy 93

Secret Key #4 - Prepare, Don't Procrastinate 93

Secret Key #5 - Test Yourself 94

General Strategies 95

    Make Predictions 95

    Answer the Question 95

    Benchmark 95

    Valid Information 95

    Avoid "Fact Traps" 96

    Milk the Question 96

    The Trap of Familiarity 96

    Eliminate Answers 96

    Tough Questions 97

    Brainstorm 97

    Read Carefully 97

    Face Value 97

Copyright © Mometrix Media. You have been licensed one copy of this document for personal use only. Any other reproduction or redistribution is strictly prohibited. All rights reserved.

LONGWOOD PUBLIC LIBRARY

Prefixes 97

Hedge Phrases 97

Switchback Words 98

New Information 98

Time Management 98

Contextual Clues 98

Don't Panic 98

Pace Yourself 98

Answer Selection 99

Check Your Work 99

Beware of Directly Quoted Answers 99

Slang 99

Extreme Statements 99

Answer Choice Families 99

Special Report: Additional Bonus Material 101

Copyright © Mometrix Media. You have been licensed one copy of this document for personal use only.
Any other reproduction or redistribution is strictly prohibited. All rights reserved.

Top 20 Test Taking Tips

1. Carefully follow all the test registration procedures
2. Know the test directions, duration, topics, question types, how many questions
3. Setup a flexible study schedule at least 3-4 weeks before test day
4. Study during the time of day you are most alert, relaxed, and stress free
5. Maximize your learning style; visual learner use visual study aids, auditory learner use auditory study aids
6. Focus on your weakest knowledge base
7. Find a study partner to review with and help clarify questions
8. Practice, practice, practice
9. Get a good night's sleep; don't try to cram the night before the test
10. Eat a well balanced meal
11. Know the exact physical location of the testing site; drive the route to the site prior to test day
12. Bring a set of ear plugs; the testing center could be noisy
13. Wear comfortable, loose fitting, layered clothing to the testing center; prepare for it to be either cold or hot during the test
14. Bring at least 2 current forms of ID to the testing center
15. Arrive to the test early; be prepared to wait and be patient
16. Eliminate the obviously wrong answer choices, then guess the first remaining choice
17. Pace yourself; don't rush, but keep working and move on if you get stuck
18. Maintain a positive attitude even if the test is going poorly
19. Keep your first answer unless you are positive it is wrong
20. Check your work, don't make a careless mistake

Copyright © Mometrix Media. You have been licensed one copy of this document for personal use only. Any other reproduction or redistribution is strictly prohibited. All rights reserved.

Pharmacology of Addictive Substances

Psychoactive chemical abuse

Psychoactive chemical abuse is a faulty adaptation pattern of behavior in which the use of chemicals has lead to some damage or pain within a twelve-month period. One of the following must be present within this time frame:

- Chemical use which is repeated and results in inability to meet Responsibilities at work, home, or school
- Chemical use which is repeated in dangerous situations such as driving
- Chemical use which is repeated and has led to legal problems such as arrest;
- Chemical use which is continued in spite of repeated problems of a social or personal nature.

Psychoactive chemical use is different from abuse in that it only occurs once. It can produce harmful effects and can lead to psychoactive chemical abuse or dependence.

Psychoactive chemical dependence

Psychoactive chemical dependence is a faulty adaptation pattern of behavior in which the use of chemicals has lead to some damage or pain within a twelve month period and is characterized by three or more of the following:

- Tolerance to the chemical is indicated by increased usage or lessened effects at the same levels of usage
- Withdrawal symptoms or the usage of similar chemicals to ward off withdrawal symptoms

- Increased amounts of the chemical are taken ,or the chemical is taken over a longer period of time
- The individual has a strong desire to cut down on the chemical use with unsuccessful results
- A great amount of time is spent getting the chemical, using the chemical, and getting over the effects
- Continued use is observed in spite of the known physical and psychological problems which occur.

Physiological dependence

Physiological dependence has to do with the body's adaptation to the presence of a chemical. When the chemical is not present, the body reacts in a negative manner, called withdrawal. The withdrawal symptoms appear in two stages.

- The first stage is called primary or acute withdrawal. It lasts from 2-7 days and is characterized by the strongest symptoms.
- The second stage is called secondary or prolonged and lasts for weeks or months.

Symptoms may include nervousness, problems sleeping, mood swings, and changes in body functions. The symptoms of the primary withdrawal are the opposite of the effects of the chemical. Immediate removal of the symptoms occurs if the chemical is taken. Detoxification is the first step of the treatment of substance abuse. The body must be cleansed from the short-term effects of the chemical before treatment can begin. Alcohol and other depressants, opiates, and cocaine require detoxification.

Copyright © Mometrix Media. You have been licensed one copy of this document for personal use only. Any other reproduction or redistribution is strictly prohibited. All rights reserved.

Psychological or behavioral dependence

Psychological or behavioral dependence refers to a person taking a chemical to satisfy a feeling or an emotional need. It is described as a craving. Usually psychological dependence appears with physiological dependence, but that is not always the case. Psychoactive chemical addicts use drugs to get pleasurable and desirable psychological effects. After some time, they may only use the chemicals to avoid the withdrawal symptoms caused by their physiological dependence. Most of the chemicals that are used by addicts cause not only a physiological but also a psychological dependence. Both physiological and psychological dependence must be present to classify an individual as psychoactive chemical dependent. Often people are prescribed psychoactive chemicals for a medical condition, and they are used properly. However, a person can become dependent because he or she likes the psychological effects that are gained from the use.

Human central nervous system

The human central nervous system is made up of three distinct parts and responsibilities:

- The central nervous system contains the brain and spinal cord. The brain has been compared to a computer and program database that contain all the pertinent information about the body. The spinal cord has been compared to a modem, acting as the connecting device between the body and the brain.
- The second main part is the peripheral nervous system, consisting of the nerves. They gather the information from all over the body and send it to the central nervous system and then receive messages.
- The third main part is the autonomic nervous system, which is entirely automatic. Its job is to make sure all of the body functions such as respiration, digestion, circulation, and reproduction do their work.

Psychoactive chemicals

The major classes of psychoactive chemicals are:
- CNS Depressants
- CNS Stimulants
- Narcotics
- Hallucinogens
- Cannabis
- Solvents/Inhalants
- Steroids
- Psychotropics

Dependent delusional system

The dependent delusional system is the way a person protects the inner person from the realization of his dependency on drugs:

- Memory and recall are one part of this system. Repression is when feelings and /or incidents are blocked from memory. A blackout is caused by drinking alcohol to a point of no active memory. Euphoric recall occurs when an addict recalls what has happened but only as he perceived it while under the influence.
- Denial is the second part of the dependent delusional system. Simple denial includes telling lies to self and others. Rationalization is using a logical excuse as a means of justification. Projecting and blaming is a way to try to make others responsible for the drug use. Intellectualizing is looking at life from an intellectual

- 7 -

Copyright © Mometrix Media. You have been licensed one copy of this document for personal use only. Any other reproduction or redistribution is strictly prohibited. All rights reserved.

view, but defying feelings and emotions.

Pharmacology and addiction counseling

The study of pharmacology is related to addiction counseling because it is important to know the nature of psychoactive chemicals, the way they affect the body and mind, and the effects of taking more than one psychoactive chemical. Further, an understanding of behaviors that are related to drug use as well as withdrawal symptoms is important. Counselors use this knowledge to help a person to get treatment and to go through recovery successfully:

- Chemical interactions - when more than one chemical is given at the same time or when a chemical is given to get the opposite effect of another chemical
- Physiological effects - physical and bio-chemical behaviors of short and long-term drug use
- Psychological effects - the effects on perception and judgment by psychoactive chemicals
- Terminology - psychoactive chemical name, brand name, and street name
- Treatment applications - refers to the purpose of detoxification and stabilization/maintenance
- Withdrawal syndrome - physical and psychological rebound effects of psychoactive chemicals

Pharmaceuticals as treatment for addiction

Healthcare professionals must be very careful about the use of pharmaceuticals when treating recovering addicts and alcoholics. Only professionals trained in substance abuse treatment should prescribe any psychoactive chemicals. Some of these chemicals can reactivate the physical and psychological dependencies and therefore cause a relapse. The following precautions should be considered before prescribing:

- Avoid any medications that contain alcohol. Examples would be cough syrup and vitamin supplements.
- Avoid any medications that contain stimulants. Examples would be appetite suppressants and antihistamines.
- Avoid any medication that contains a narcotic. Examples would be anti-diarrheals and pain relievers.
- Avoid any medication that contains a depressant or a sedative-hypnotic.
- Confer with a pharmacist or M.D. regarding alternative methods.

Disease Model of Addiction

Elements of the Disease Model of Addiction are:

- Addiction is a biopsysocial disease
- A genetic predisposition to the disease has been proven;
- Tolerance to drugs is built up
- Addicts and alcoholics who have family histories of addiction show more antisocial behavior
- Psychological addiction occurs before physical addiction and is present long after detoxification

Elements of psychological addiction are as follows:

- Psychological primacy--the need to get drugs is the most important thing in life
- Self doubt--being able to function is not possible without drugs
- Relationship to the drug--life is not worthwhile without the drug

- 8 -

Copyright © Mometrix Media. You have been licensed one copy of this document for personal use only. Any other reproduction or redistribution is strictly prohibited. All rights reserved.

- Inability to abstain--cannot stop using the drug caused by cravings, preoccupation with the drug, remembering how good it felt and feelings of frustration and depression when not using
- Inability to control the amount used

Additional elements of the Disease Model are
- Personality changes
- Conflicted behavior

Central nervous system depressants

Central nervous system depressants are normally used as sedative-hypnotics. CNS depressants are the most widely used psychoactive chemicals in medicine. The first drug in this group to be invented was phenobarbital (1850). These drugs can depress certain body functions without affecting the rest. Sedatives lose their effectiveness after a very short period of time. Their main effect is one of sedation and drowsiness. The drugs are taken orally or injected in a water mix. Dependence and tolerance of central nervous system depressants is moderate to high physical dependence, low to moderate tolerance, and moderate to high psychological dependence. Symptoms include drunken behavior, confusion, drowsiness, hostility, irritability, poor judgment, and paranoid thinking. Side effects include tolerance, short-lived usefulness, depression, withdrawal, released inhibition and hostility, agitation, and habit-formation.

Types of drugs include:
- Alcohol - ethyl alcohol ethanol in the form of beer, liquor, wine
- Barbiturates - Amytal, Nembutal, Phenobarbital, Seconal, Tuinal
- Benzodiazepines - Valium, Librium, Ativan, Serax, Xanax, Tranxene, Klonopin

- Other - Ambien, Chloral Hydrate, Doriden, Mepobamate, Noludar, Paraldehyde, Placidyl, Quaaludes

The stages of withdrawal from CNS depressants are as follows:
- Stage 1--characterized by shakes. 90% of patients experience flushed face, nausea, irritability, loss of appetite, short-term memory loss, nervousness, insomnia, mild disorientation, and inability to sleep. The worst usually occurs from 24-36 hours after the last drink.
- Stage 2--characterized by hallucinations. About 25% of patients experience perception disturbances from shadows and movements. In addition, objects can look distorted or unreal.
- Stage 3--characterized by seizures. Patients may experience Grand Mal seizures, which means full body seizures. The seizures most often occur between 7 and 48 hours after the last drink.
- Stage 4--characterized by Delirium Tremens (DTs). Patients can experience agitation, hallucinations, fever, dilated pupils, delusions, extreme confusion, sleep disorders, tremors, profuse sweating, and tachycardia. DTs usually occur in 3 to 5 days after the last drink.

The withdrawal effects are almost the exact opposite of the pharmacological use. Withdrawal symptoms usually include anxiety, shaking, agitation, restlessness, and sweating. Early symptoms are not usually dangerous. One of the most dangerous effects is the depression of the respiratory system if the sedative is used in conjunction with alcohol.

Copyright © Mometrix Media. You have been licensed one copy of this document for personal use only. Any other reproduction or redistribution is strictly prohibited. All rights reserved.

CNS depressant barbiturates by chemical name and trade name are:

- Amobarbital (Amytal)
- Aprobarbital (Alurate)
- Butabarbital (Butalan, butisol, Sarisol No. 2)
- Mephobarbital (Mebaral)
- Metharbital (Gemonil) - Not available in U.S.
- Pentobarbital (Nembutal)
- Phenobarbital (Barbita, Luminal, Solfoton)
- Secobarbital (Seconal)

Method of administration are oral, IV, and IM. Short term effects include inducing sleep, muscle relaxation, and calming anxiety. Long-term effects include nausea/vomiting, constipation, bradycardia, high blood pressure, insomnia, anxiety, confusion, apnea, hypoventilation, nightmares, ataxia, dizziness, hallucinations, and abnormal thinking. Babies born to mothers who have used barbiturates in the last trimester will experience withdrawal.

CNS depressant benzodiazepines by chemical and trade name are:

- Alprazolam (Xanax) - intermediate acting
- Bromazepam (Lectopam) Not available in U.S. intermediate acting
- Chlordiazepoxide (Libritabs, Librium, Lipoxide)- long acting
- Clonazepam (Klonopin)- long acting
- Clorazepate (Gen-XENE, Tranxene-SD, Tranxene T-Tab)- long acting
- Diazepam (Diazepam Intensol, T-Quil, Valium, Valrelease, Vazepam, Zetran)-long acting
- Estazolam (ProSom)- intermediate acting
- Flurazepam (Dalmane, Durapam)- long acting

- Halazepam (Paxipam)- intermediate acting
- Ketazolam (Loftran) Not available in U.S.-possibly long acting
- Lorazepam (Alzapam, Ativan, Larazepam Intensol)- intermediate acting
- Midazolam (Versed) - short acting
- Nitrazepam (Mogadon) Not available in U.S.- possibly long acting
- Oxazepam (Serax)- intermediate acting
- Prazepam (Centrax)- possibly long acting
- Quazepam (Doral)- possibly long acting
- Temazepam (Razepam, Restoril)- intermediate acting
- Triazolam (Halcion) - short acting

Short-term effects include anti-anxiety and sedative effects. Mazicon is a benzodiazepine antagonist.

Alcohol

Alcohol is a sedative because is depresses the central nervous system. Effects of use are lowering of inhibitions, relaxation, and the inhibition of good judgment. Alcohol comes in two forms. One is ethyl alcohol, found in beer, wine, and liquor. Methyl alcohol is found in paint removers, antifreeze, solvents, and some other household products. It is completely poisonous. The effects of alcohol vary from person to person. Alcohol causes the peripheral blood vessels to dilate and increases the heart rate. It also decreases reaction time and fine muscle coordination. Tolerance to alcohol can develop. Sudden stopping of alcohol use can cause withdrawal symptoms such as edginess, insomnia, poor appetite, and/or sweating. Severe symptoms may include hallucinations, tremors, convulsions and pain.

Copyright © Mometrix Media. You have been licensed one copy of this document for personal use only. Any other reproduction or redistribution is strictly prohibited. All rights reserved.

Short and long-term effects

Short-term effects of drinking alcohol include a feeling of euphoria, drowsiness, dizziness, and a flushing of the complexion. Driving is impaired as well as other coordination skills. All of these occur after only a few drinks. A few more drinks effect vision, speech and balance. Alcohol should not be taken with any other drugs because it can change the way the other drug acts within the body. Overdrinking can result in what is known as a "hangover", or withdrawal from alcohol. Headaches, nausea, shakiness, as well as short-term memory loss can occur.

Long-term heavy usage can result in stomach ulcers, liver damage, sexual problems, brain damage, and even cancer. It can also affect family relationships and work performance.

Withdrawal syndrome and treatment

There are two stages for the alcohol withdrawal syndrome. During these stages there is a potential for the withdrawal to be a threat to life. Characteristics of Stage 1 are:

- Increase in blood pressure, pulse, and temperature.
- Limited attention span, state of anxiety, sleeplessness
- Nausea and vomiting, shakes, speech is slurred, walking is unsteady, frequent urination.

Characteristics of Stage 2 are:

- Hallucinations evidenced by fearful state, distraction, and/or
- Disorientation Large seizure such as Grand Mal is possible.
- DTs develop which are evidenced by an extreme agitated state, confusion, incontinence, extreme psychomotor activity, talking to people who are not there, and uncooperative behavior.

Treatment applications include increase sedation; monitor fluids, electrolytes, and vital signs; observe and provide a quiet, well-lit room. Do not try to reason with the patient or provide any therapy; act with kindness and gentleness; behave calmly; orient patient back to reality; no moralizing or blaming; and close doors to cut down on shadows.

Detoxification

Alcohol detoxification is usually provided in a hospital setting and does not normally last longer than five days. Access to medical supervision is important so that nutrition, fluid and electrolyte level, and medications can be provided.

After a patient has gone through withdrawal, he may still experience disturbances with eating and sleeping, uncontrollable shakes, sweating, hallucinating, agitated behavior, and clouded senses. There may also be an elevation in temperature and pulse rate and convulsions can even occur.

Outpatient detoxification treatment does exist, but it is not nearly as successful as inpatient treatment. Benzodiazepines and other CNS depressants such as barbiturates may be helpful, in addition to medications that help minimize tremors, rapid heart rate, and high blood pressure.

Pharmacotherapies for dependence

Pharmacotherapies available for alcohol dependence are:

- Disulfiram (Antabuse) - This medication makes people sick if they use alcohol. It must be used every day, which may be difficult for some patients. Its effectiveness as a treatment is very good because most alcoholics do not drink while taking it because of the effects produced. The treatment of opiate/alcoholic

Copyright © Mometrix Media. You have been licensed one copy of this document for personal use only. Any other reproduction or redistribution is strictly prohibited. All rights reserved.

addicts is very successful also due to the fact that Disulfiram and Methadone can be taken together. Another good point for the use of Disulfiram is that it can be used in the workplace or in a treatment program connected to parole/probation or work release.

- Naltrexone - Naltrexone was once known as Trexan but now is called ReVia. It works by reducing the craving mechanism for alcohol. Other steps can be taken in conjunction with the use of Naltrexone that increase the effectiveness of treatment. These steps include development of coping skills, prevention of relapse, and the use of support groups.

Health disorders related to abuse

Gastrointestinal health disorders related to alcohol abuse include:

- Esophagitis--inflammation of the esophagus
- Esophageal carcinoma--cancer of the esophagus
- Gastritis--inflammation of the mucous membrane of the stomach
- Malabsorption--poor or defective absorption of nutrients from the intestinal tract
- Chronic diarrhea
- Pancreatitis--inflammation of the pancreas
- Fatty liver--reduces liver function
- Alcoholic hepatitis--liver disease
- Cirrhosis--liver disease which results in loss of function of liver cells

Cardiovascular health disorders related to alcohol abuse include:

- Hypertension--high blood pressure
- Alcoholic cardiomyopathy--an abnormal condition of the heart muscle

- Beriberi--a nutritional deficiency disease

Pulmonary health disorders include:

- Emphysema--disease of the lungs in which the size of air spaces increase, resulting in labored breathing
- Carcinoma

Skin health disorders include:

- Rosacea--chronic skin condition caused by constant dilation of the capillaries
- Telangiectasia--skin condition caused by chronic dilation of the Capillaries
- Rhinophyma--abnormal enlargement of the nose

Neurologic and psychiatric disorders include:

- Peripheral neuropathy--disease affecting cranial or spinal nerves
- Convulsive disorders
- Hallucinations
- Delirium tremens

Barbiturates

Withdrawal syndrome and drug interactions

The most dangerous part of barbiturate withdrawal is the possibility of the occurrence of blood pressure and breathing problems. They must be treated immediately or the situation can become life threatening. Normal symptoms of the withdrawal syndrome include nausea and vomiting, increased heart rate, sweating, abdominal cramping, and shakes. There are incidents during peak withdrawal of severe seizures, uncontrolled heartbeat, delirium, and even death.

Some drugs when mixed with barbiturates can be potentially dangerous. Phenobarbital has shown the

- 12 -

Copyright © Mometrix Media. You have been licensed one copy of this document for personal use only. Any other reproduction or redistribution is strictly prohibited. All rights reserved.

highest occurrence. The following fall into this group: Anticoagulants such as Dicumarol, warfarin, acenocoumaral, and Phenprocoumon, Corticosteroids, Guseofulvin, Doxycycline, Phenytoin, sodium valproate, valporic acid, CNS depressants, Mono amino oxidase inhibitors, Estradiol, estrone, progesterone, and other steroidal hormones.

<u>Treatment applications</u>
Detoxification for barbiturates must take place under medical supervision because of the high risk for life-threatening episodes. It is important to determine if any other drugs are being used. Addiction counselors need to be educated regarding the long-term withdrawal symptoms characteristic of this group of drugs. The client's treatment plan needs to include extended care because his education and performance capabilities are impaired during the normal treatment stay. Client education about barbiturates is necessary. Education of his family is necessary also. The need for a support system should be stressed. Coping skills and decision-making skills should be taught. Alternative ways to relax and get to sleep should be introduced. Ways to work with shame, fear, and grief should be taught to help the client to move toward sobriety. Education of the patient's physician is a necessary component too.

Benzodiazepines and sedatives

Benzodiazepines and sedatives are different in several ways. Benzodiazepines, known as Bzs, are usually known as tranquilizers.
- They are useful in reducing anxiety. Bzs target anxiety rather than being general depressants.
- Less drowsiness and physical impairment than sedatives has been noted.

- Also, they are safer to take than sedatives. Even taking large amounts of the drug at one time do not produce the fatal results of sedatives.
- A further difference is that the effect of reducing anxiety is felt for a much longer time than is seen with sedatives.

Doctors are much more prone to prescribe Bzs today than sedatives. Bzs are not only effective for reducing anxiety, but they are also very good sleeping pills.

Tranquilizers

Tranquilizers belong to a group of drugs known as benzodiazepines. These are prescription drugs given to help relieve anxiety and tension prior to surgery and to treat some of the side effects of alcohol withdrawal. Some of the brand names of well-known tranquilizers are Valium, Librium, Ativan and Serax. Valium (diazepam) is the best-known street drug because it is easy to attain and provides a moderate high. Although it is very dangerous, some users combine alcohol with Valium, which also depresses the central nervous system. Sedatives, such as sleeping pills, are also part of this group of substances. They are part of the barbiturate family of drugs.

<u>Short and long-term effects</u>
Short-term effects of tranquilizer use are reduced anxiety and tension, calmness, drowsiness and slight problems with memory and thinking. Fatigue, reduced inhibition, and clumsiness have also been noted. When people use tranquilizers, they should not drive or operate machinery.

Long-term effects include headaches, lack of energy, irritability, and sexual problems. Abuse of tranquilizers can

Copyright © Mometrix Media. You have been licensed one copy of this document for personal use only. Any other reproduction or redistribution is strictly prohibited. All rights reserved.

cause problems with memory, thinking, judgment, muscle weakness, slurring of speech, anxiety, and insomnia to name a few. An overdose of tranquilizers can even cause coma. Abuse or long-term use of tranquilizers can develop strong cravings for the drug. Other effects include muscle weakness, anxiety, insomnia, and problems with judgment and thinking.

CNS Stimulants

CNS stimulants by chemical and trade name are:
- Synthetic Amphetamines, D,L-amphetamine (Benzedrine, Obetrol, Biphetamine), Dextroamphetamine (Dexedrine, Eskatrol)
- Dextromethamphetamine base (None), Levo amphetamine (Vick's Inhaler), Methamphetamine (Methadrine, Desoxyn)
- Amphetamine Congeners (diet pills), Diethylpropion (Tenuate, Tepanil), Methcathinone (None), Methylphenidate (Ritalin)
- Phenmetrazine (Preludin), Phentermine HCL (Fastin, Adipex)
- Phentermine resin (Bontril, Melfiat, Pendiet, Phenazine, Plegine, Statobex, Trimtabs), Pemoline (Cylert), Caffeine
- Chocolate (Hershey...), Coffee (Columbia, French Roast...)
- Colas (Coca Cola, Pepsi...), Ephedrine (No Doz, Alert, Vivarin)
- Phenylpropanolamine (No Doz, Alert, Vivarin), Tea (Lipton....)
- Cocaine
- Cocaine HCL> hydrochloride, Freebase cocaine
- Nicotine
- Chewing tobacco (Day's Work), Cigarettes, cigars (Marlboro)
- Pipe tobacco (Sir Walter Raleigh), Snuff (Copenhagen)

Method of use are nasal, injection, and smoking. Short-term side effects include loss of appetite, increased motor and speech activity, pupils are dilated, dry mouth, insomnia, anxiousness, increase in blood pressure and heart rate, irritability, excitability, and paranoia.

History of use
The use and abuse of stimulants has been around for a long time. As far back as 400 years ago, cocaine was being used. Today, cocaine is the most popular psychochemical in use; however the method of administration differs from early use. The manufacture of crack cocaine and the self-administration method of free-basing (which allows the drug to enter the body in a pure state) create a strong demand for the drug. This situation makes it very difficult to combat. Other drugs in the category of stimulants such as Ritalin and the amphetamines do not have as long a history because they are man-made. The use of amphetamines was stopped in both Japan and Sweden because of strict control and mandated treatment. In the U.S. the same pattern is being seen because amphetamine prescriptions are being prohibited or strongly controlled in many states.

Withdrawal effects
The withdrawal effects from stimulants are almost the direct opposite of the effects of use. Some of these effects are depression, increase in appetite, irritability, weakness and energy loss, increased need for sleep, and loss of concentration. More serious side effects can be produced, however. Some of the same symptoms as seen in paranoid schizophrenia are observed such as suspicion, fears, hallucinations and delusions. Seizures can also be produced which can cause heart toxicity and sudden death.

Copyright © Mometrix Media. You have been licensed one copy of this document for personal use only. Any other reproduction or redistribution is strictly prohibited. All rights reserved.

Classes of stimulants

There are three classes of stimulant drugs - amphetamines, naturally occurring, and synthetic agents like amphetamines. The synthetic amphetamines are D, L-amphetamine, Dextroamphetamine, and Methamphetamine. Naturally occurring drugs are caffeine, cocaine, and nicotine. The synthetic agents like amphetamines are Diethylpropion, Methylphenidate, Pemoline, Phenmetrazine, Phentermine HCL, Phentermine resin. Methods of use include snorting (nasal), which is longer acting; shooting (injected), which is most intense; and free-basing (smoking), which is intense and rapid. These drugs are both physically and psychologically addictive, and a tolerance is developed. User symptoms include increased motor and speech activity, increased blood pressure and heart rate, irritable, anxious, dilated pupils, dry mouth, and insomnia. Detoxification medications include Bromocriptine (Parlodel) and Amantadine (Symmetrel) for decreasing cocaine cravings. Antidepressants used are Desipramine (Norpramin) and Imipramine.

Amphetamines

Amphetamines are in a class of drugs known as stimulants. They act much like adrenalin in the body and are therefore known as speed, uppers, or bennies. Medically, amphetamines are used to treat narcolepsy, that is, uncontrolled sleep episodes. They are also used to treat hyperactive children. Ritalin is one of the drugs in this group. In the past, amphetamines were used to treat obesity as well as depression, but now it is against the law to use them for these purposes. As with other drugs, the more a person takes, the more the body needs to get the same effects. Dependence on amphetamines, even low dosages, develops over time. Withdrawal symptoms include fatigue, interrupted sleep patterns, an increase in appetite and moderate to severe depression.

Short and long-term effects

Short-term effects of amphetamines use vary from person to person. An increase in the level of blood sugar, inability to sleep, an increase in alertness and tremors are all possible. Other side effects might include diarrhea, rapid heartbeat, increase in urine output, dry mouth, or rapid breathing. Higher dose usage can produce panic, depression or irritability. Euphoric feelings along with unreal perceptions of personal strength or intelligence can occur in some individuals.

Long-term effects related to regular use include insomnia, elevated blood pressure, skin rashes, and irregular heart beat. Eating disorders and nutritional problems result from the appetite-suppressant effect of amphetamines. If an individual uses high doses of amphetamines over a long period of time, mental problems, such as chronic psychosis, which is like paranoid schizophrenia, can develop.

Methamphetamines

Methamphetamines are chemically made stimulants. They are related to amphetamines but the effects are much greater. They are made in illegal home labs. They are known on the street as speed, meth, and chalk.
Methamphetamine hydrochloride looks like ice crystals which can be smoked. This type is known as ice, crystal, glass, and tina on the street.
Methamphetamines can be injected, taken orally, snorted, or smoked. Its use is quickly and highly addictive. Smoking or injection causes a "high" or "rush" that is very pleasurable. Snorting or oral use produces a euphoric high, but no rush. The use of methamphetamines cause decreased appetite, increased respiration,

Copyright © Mometrix Media. You have been licensed one copy of this document for personal use only. Any other reproduction or redistribution is strictly prohibited. All rights reserved.

insomnia, euphoria, irritability, tremors, anxiety, and many other symptoms.

Crack

"Crack" is made from cocaine powder and is called "rock" on the street. When cocaine is treated with common household products, it changes into solid chunks. It is heated with baking soda until the water evaporates, which causes a cracking sound. Smoking crack provides a quicker rush than sniffing or snorting cocaine powder. The use of crack creates euphoria, often described as a whole body orgasm. This euphoric state is followed by a crash, which includes anxiety, paranoia, and extreme fatigue. These symptoms, together with a very strong craving for the drug, reinforce a desire to use again.

Short and long-term effects
Short-term effects of crack use may include a feeling of euphoria and high energy, decrease in appetite, and an increase in heart rate and body temperature. Large doses can cause convulsions, nausea, blood pressure elevations, twitching, and fever. Overdosing on crack can result in respiratory failure caused by seizures, stroke and/or heart failure, which can lead to death.

The long-term effects of crack include constipation, insomnia, impotence, and/or weight loss. Lung damage is also a possibility due to inhalation of the vapors. Addiction to the drug can be a result of regular use. Because crack users get an intense high in a very short amount of time, followed by feelings of deep depression, addiction often results.

Cocaine

Cocaine looks like a fine white powder. It is a stimulant to the central nervous system. It stimulates the brain to release dopamine and norepinephrine, causing a euphoric state. Effects can be felt within 30 seconds after use. On the street, cocaine is known as coke, snow, flake or stardust. When sold, it is often mixed with cornstarch, icing sugar, talcum powder, or laxatives. It is also mixed with benzocaine, providing a numbing effect. Users inject or sniff cocaine, or they can smoke it, which is known as "free basing". Doctors use it as a local anesthetic. Tolerance to cocaine builds after a period of time, requiring increasing amounts to get the same effect. The drug is addictive. Some withdrawal symptoms are fatigue, depression, anger, confusion, irritability, strong craving for cocaine, and restless sleep.

Short and long-term effects
Short-term effects of cocaine use can include dilation of the pupils, rapid heart rate and breathing, sweating and heightened alertness, feeling of confidence and well-being. A decrease in appetite can also occur. Heavy usage effects are blurred vision, high blood pressure, hallucinations, violent behavior, muscle spasms, loss of coordination, stroke, nausea, twitching, fever, and chest pain. Many users may experience stuffy noses and/or insomnia.

The long-term effects of regular usage are hallucinations, weight loss, impotence, difficulty urinating, constipation, insomnia, restlessness, excitability and a suspicious nature. These users are lethargic, apathetic, and cannot sleep, which may lead to abuse of other drugs to alleviate these symptoms. Chronic sniffing characteristics include stuffy or runny nose, nasal bleeding or chapped nostrils.

Bingeing and detoxification
Cocaine users usually follow a pattern of bingeing and withdrawal. The binge lasts from 12 to 36 hours during which the use is continual. Then the drugs run out and

Copyright © Mometrix Media. You have been licensed one copy of this document for personal use only. Any other reproduction or redistribution is strictly prohibited. All rights reserved.

withdrawal takes place and detoxification occurs. Some of the effects of withdrawal are increased appetite, depression, weakness, irritability, excessive sleepiness, decreased ability to experience pleasure, lack of concentration, and paranoid ideation. The user also has a craving for the drug, usually resulting in another round of use. Detoxification in a supervised atmosphere has the goal of managing the symptoms and cravings long enough to break up the binge/craving cycle. Helpful drugs are desipramine HCL, amantadine, bromocriptine, flupenthixol decanoate, and buprenorphine.

Treatment and pharmacotherapies
Treatment for any kind of stimulant abuse is very difficult because of the high reward effects of the drug use. Users should get into a support group just for narcotics and cocaine abusers rather than AA because of the different ways they are affected. Cocaine users are not eager to seek treatment because using has such reinforcing qualities and abstaining is so intense. Using caffeine, diet pills and nicotine during treatment can trigger cravings and the patient can end up in relapse. Certain things need to be addressed during therapy: changing language and habits along with activities and places to go; and stimulating the mind and body through exercise and activities other than looking for cocaine. Nutritional counseling is another important component of treatment. No real pharmacotherapies have been developed for cocaine users. It is possible that some antidepressants and medications that are used for treating Parkinson's disease may be helpful. The most effective treatment is psychotherapeutic treatment and regular urine monitoring.

Caffeine

Caffeine is found in coffee, tea, chocolate, and cola products. It can also be found in some pain relievers. Caffeine is a stimulant that blocks the inhibitory receptors for the neurotransmitter adenosine. Also, caffeine inhibits certain enzymes that cause an increase in brain activity. Dependence does develop for the chemical. Caffeine does cause an increase in heartbeat and respiration. Withdrawal effects are noticed upon the stopping of caffeine use. Some of these such as the headache are not pleasant. Caffeine is not only physically addictive but also psychologically addictive. Moderate use has not been shown to be dangerous. It can also help to minimize migraine headaches because caffeine causes the blood vessels in the brain to constrict.

Narcotics

There are three classes of narcotics-- naturally occurring, semisynthetic, and synthetic. Examples of naturally occurring narcotics are Codeine, Morphine, Opium, and Thebaine. Semisynthetic narcotics are Dilaudid, Heroin, and Percodan. Synthetic narcotic examples include Darvon, Demerol, Fentanyl, and Methadone. These drugs are used by injecting (I.V. or skin popping), oral administration, or smoking (Opium). Physical and psychological dependence are very rapid and very high. A tolerance is also developed. Users have the following symptoms: nausea, constipation, drowsiness, slurring speech and nodding of head, pinpoint pupils, euphoria, and flushed face, neck and chest.

Withdrawal
Withdrawal symptoms from narcotics are just the opposite from the user effects. The symptoms appear in the following order:

Copyright © Mometrix Media. You have been licensed one copy of this document for personal use only. Any other reproduction or redistribution is strictly prohibited. All rights reserved.

- feeling uneasy with anxiety about approaching withdrawal
- restlessness
- runny nose and teary eyes
- nausea with diarrhea
- pupils are dilated
- cramping in the stomach
- vomiting

Some individuals with severe withdrawal experience a development of bumps (gooseflesh) on the skin. Symptoms normally begin slowly and then increase in intensity following by a gradual subsiding. This usually lasts from 2-5 days after the last dose. These symptoms can occur on the job if the individual does not get to use the narcotic on time. Often, the drugs are brought to work so that the individual is not thrown into withdrawal. Narcotic antagonists include Naloxone (Narcan) and Naltrexone (ReVia). Narcan is used to treat overdose, and ReVia is used to treat narcotic dependence. Residual withdrawal, or a "protracted abstinence syndrome," is characterized by an inability to handle stress, decreased threshold for pain, and not being able to overcome tiredness, discomfort, and weakness.

Drug interaction and treatment
Several narcotics are mixed with other drugs. Examples are the combination of Talwin and antihistamines, which is called "T" & Blues. This mixture is injected. Another example is Dilaudid and Cocaine which is called "Speedballs". A common mixture is that of Codeine and cough syrup which is a medical treatment for pain and coughing.

Some successful treatment programs are Therapeutic Communities (Synanon), Methadone Maintenance, and the use of former addicts in group therapy. Methadone is a chemical used to stabilize a patient during withdrawal and is addictive itself. However there are other

chemical non-addicting antagonists. The most effective treatment seems to be therapy, group support and court sanctions. Coping skills need to be taught to narcotic addicts along with changes in lifestyle and behavior.

Methadone maintenance programs
When methadone is used in the proper dosage, time frame, and as part of a rehab program, it is the most effective treatment for heroin addicts. It helps relieve the uncomfortable symptoms of withdrawal and also prevents heroin use during treatment due to a mechanism called cross tolerance. There have been some problems in methadone programs such as polydrug use (cocaine and alcohol) and misuse of the methadone when it was taken at home. LAAM was developed to help with these problems. Addicts were able to come in three times a week to get their methadone. None was taken home. Also, a drug causing an adverse effect if alcohol was used with methadone could be given. Methadone programs have helped a great deal with the spread of AIDS. Also, the cost involved in the treatment of addicts has been reduced. Employment has been improved and crime reduced.

Naltrexone
Naltrexone, an opiate blocker, has been found to be effective in the treatment of heroin addicts. Two problems do exist in its use:
- Detoxification must be completed before Naltrexone can be started.
- Its use requires patient compliance after detox.

The first problem has been partially solved by the use of clonidine plus naltrexone during detox, which shortens detox considerably. The probation system has made patient compliance not such a problem by requiring Naltrexone to be taken three times a week as a

Copyright © Mometrix Media. You have been licensed one copy of this document for personal use only. Any other reproduction or redistribution is strictly prohibited. All rights reserved.

condition of parole or a work/release program. This is working very well because they do not want to go back to prison. Also, Naltrexone totally blocks any of the effects of heroin.

Chemical and trade names
NARCOTICS by chemical and trade names are:

- Opiates Poppy extracts: Codeine (Empirin with codeine, Tylenol with codeine), Diacetyl morphine (Heroin), Hydrocodone (Hycodan, Vicodin), Hydromorphone (Dilaudid), Morphine (Various), Opium (Laudanum, Pantopon, Paregoric), Oxycodone (Percodan, Percocet, Tylox)
- Opioids
- Synthetic opiates: Fentanyl (Sublimaze), Hydrocodonebitartrate/acetamin ophen (Lorcet, Lortab), L acetyl alpha methadol (LAAM), Levorphanol (Levorphanol), Levomethadyl acetate hydrochloride (Orlaam), Meperidine (Demerol), Methadone (Dolophine), Pentazocine (Talwin), Propoxyphene (Darvon, Darvocet-N)

Opiate narcotics

Opiate narcotics are usually thought of as pain-killing drugs or analgesics. These drugs have the potential to cause addiction. The physical symptom of use is an intense feeling of well-being and euphoria. Opiate narcotics can be divided into two groups--naturally occurring and synthetic. Morphine and codeine are in the natural group. They are obtained from the opium poppy. Heroin is made chemically from morphine. Demerol (meperidine), Talwin (pentazocine), and Methadone are made in a laboratory so they are included in the synthetic group.

Symptoms of withdrawal for an opiate user include stomach cramps, diarrhea, runny nose, tears, yawning, goose bumps, and a general sense of insecurity. These symptoms lessen in severity in a few days, but may take weeks or months to completely subside.

Short and long-term effects
Short-term effects of opiate use depend on amount taken, the individual's mood prior to usage, other drug usage and even the environment. Opiates depress the central nervous system but stimulate the brain centers. This causes a rush of great pleasure after the drug is injected. Short-term side effects can include nausea, constipation and drowsiness. These can occur with low dosages of the drug. High dosages can cause severe respiratory system problems. Clammy, blue skin, pupils that look like pin pricks and dry mouth are also indicative of higher dose usage. Overdose can cause coma or death due to suppressed breathing.

Long-term effects can include a decrease in sexual drive, menstrual irregularity, and constipation. If the drugs are injected, liver disease, AIDS and infections related to dirty needles can occur.

Hallucinogens

Hallucinogens by chemical name and ingredients are:

- Anticholinergics, Atrophine, belladonna, datura, jimsonweed, scopolamine, thornapple, wolfbane
- Indole Psychedelics
- DMT Dimethltryptamine, Ibota plant (ingredient: Ibogaine)
- LSD (ingredient: Lysergic acid diethylamide), Morning glory Seeds and Hawaiian Woodrose (ingredient: Lysergic acid amide),Mushrooms (ingredient:

Copyright © Mometrix Media. You have been licensed one copy of this document for personal use only. Any other reproduction or redistribution is strictly prohibited. All rights reserved.

Psilocybin), Yage (ingredient: Harmaline and DMT)
- Phenylethylamine Psychedelics
- MDA, MMDA, MDM, MDE, etc. 2CB (ingredient: variations of Methylenedioxy 4, bromo dimenthoxy phenethylamine) , STP, (DO"M) (ingredient: 4methyl 2,5 dimethoxyamphetamine), STP-LSD Combo - synthetic (ingredient: dimethoxamphetamine with LSD), U4Euh (ingredient: 4 methylaminorex)
- Other Psychedelics
- Amanita mushrooms - fly agaric (ingredients: Ibotenic acid, muscimol)
- Kava root (ingredient: Alpha pryones), Nutmeg and mace (ingredient: Myristicin)
- PCP (ingredient: Phencycllidine)

PCP
PCP, better known as phencyclidine, is most widely recognized as a hallucinogen. However, it can also act as a stimulant as well as a painkiller. PCP comes in several forms. It can be a powder, a liquid, or a tablet. These different forms can be smoked, swallowed or injected. Often it is combined with other substances such as LSD and marijuana. On the street PCP is known as "angel dust". It has been used medically as an anesthetic on humans as well as horses. Its use on horses earned it the street name of "horse tranquilizer". PCP users can build up a tolerance to the drug so that more and more is needed to achieve the same effects. Users also become dependent and develop strong cravings for the drug, although symptoms vary from person to person and with each use of the drug.

The short-term effects of PCP use vary greatly from person to person because it can act as both a stimulant and a depressant. Some individuals find it difficult to concentrate and communicate. Some may even have a sense of separation from their surroundings. Confusion is not unusual even to the extent of unreal perceptions of time, space, and body images.

Not much is known about the long-term effects of PCP use because there are so few regular users. The known effects include speech problems, memory loss, depression and anxiety. Flashbacks can occur days or even months after use. These flashbacks may include hallucinations and sensations felt during PCP use. Other long-term effects include withdrawal from people and relationships as well as crippling anxiety. Users also develop symptoms very much like schizophrenia or violent paranoia.

LSD
LSD belongs to the drug family of hallucinogens. It is such a strong drug that the amount of LSD the size of an aspirin would equal 3000 doses. On the street LSD is called "acid". The white powder can be bought in capsules or tablets. These are completely colorless and tasteless. Also, LSD can be put into candy, cookies or absorbed into paper, postage stamps, and ink blotters. No deaths have been linked to overdoses of LSD. However, it has been tied to suicides, accidental deaths, murder and wounds which were self-inflicted. Tolerance to LSD builds in the same way as most other drugs. Increasing amounts are required to get the same effect. The effects do have a peak at which time they do not get any stronger or more vivid, but the damages to the body do increase.

Short-term effects of LSD use begin within a few minutes after use and can last as long as 12 hours. LSD affects the central nervous system. Sight and hearing can be affected as well as the sense of taste. It causes an increase in blood pressure, dilated pupils, nausea, chills and fever,

Copyright © Mometrix Media. You have been licensed one copy of this document for personal use only. Any other reproduction or redistribution is strictly prohibited. All rights reserved.

numbness, and rapid heartbeat. Memory can be affected. Long-term memory is exceptionally clear and strong, although short-term memory is almost non-existent.

Long-term effects of LSD use are most often manifested in flashbacks. All of the short-term effects of the drug are experienced all over again. This can happen even if no LSD has been taken for months. Use by pregnant women can cause birth defects or even miscarriage. Some heavy users are characterized by apathy, no interest in the future and very little patience or ability to cope with frustrations. They also run the risk of developing chronic psychosis.

Cannabis

Cannabis is made from the leaves and flowers of a plant called cannabis saliva. It is a mood-altering drug. Marijuana, hashish and hash oil are forms of cannabis. The mood-altering effects are caused by the presence of THC (delta-9-tetrahydrocannabinol). Hash oil contains up to 60 percent THC whereas marijuana contains 7 to 15 percent. Cannabis is usually smoked but can be put into food and eaten. The high created by cannabis use can last up to two to three hours. A marijuana cigarette is called a joint. Users can become dependent on cannabis. The body also develops a tolerance to the drug. Withdrawal symptoms last for about a week but are not severe, although cravings for the drug may not go away that quickly. The idea that marijuana use leads to harder drug use has not been proven.

Short and long-term effects
Short-term effects of cannabis use are relaxation and lowered inhibition after just a few puffs. The user might become very talkative or very quiet. There is an increase in sharpness of the senses, and plain everyday items take on special meanings or properties. Attention span and concentration can become shorter. Judging distance becomes difficult. Time passage has little meaning. Other effects may include red eyes, drowsiness, balance problems, increased appetite, and dry mouth.

Long-term effects include damage to lungs as with cigarettes. Marijuana cigarettes contain four times as much tar as regular cigarettes so the danger of lung cancer is increased. Other long-term effects can include apathy, failure to set goals, difficulty in performing simple tasks, neglect of personal appearance, slow mental responses, and difficulty with speech.

Inhalants

Inhalants are vapors that are inhaled in order to produce mind-altering effects. These vapors are chemicals most often found in household products. Inhalants slow the body down as well as producing intoxication. Examples of inhalants include paint thinners or removers, gasoline, glue, felt tip pens, spray paint, hair spray and gases in butane lighters. They are known on the street as whippets, poppers, and snappers. Inhalation from vapors from these products can cause hearing loss, bone marrow, central nervous system and brain damage, and limb spasms. Liver and kidney damage as well as blood oxygen depletion can also occur.

Inhalants used in drug abuse and their sources are:
- Organic Solvents and Sprays--
  - Acetone (found in polish remover),
  - Butane (found in fuel gas)
  - Butane, isopropane (lighter fluid),

Copyright © Mometrix Media. You have been licensed one copy of this document for personal use only. Any other reproduction or redistribution is strictly prohibited. All rights reserved.

- o Butane, propane, fluorocarbons (hair sprays, deodorants),
- o Ethyl chloride (local anesthetic),
- o Fluorocarbons (analgesic/asthma sprays),
- Gasoline - leaded or unleaded (gasoline)
- Tetrachloroethylene, trichloroethane trichloroethylene (dry cleaning fluid, spot removers, correction fluid),
- Toluene, butane, propane, fluorocarbons, hydrocarbons (spray paint), Toluene, hexane, nethyl chloride, acetone, methyl ethyl ketone, methyl butyl, ketone (airplane glue)
- Toluene, methylene chloride, methanol (paint removers/thinners)
- Trichloroethylene (PVC cement)
- Nitrous oxide--found in whipped cream propellant - street names: whippets, laughing gas, blue num, nitrous
- Isoamyl nitrate, Isobutyl nitrate, Isopropyl nitrate--found in room Deodorizers; street names: Locker Room, Rush, Quicksilver, Bolt, Poppers
- Other anesthetics:
  - o Chloroform
  - o Ether

Anabolic-androgenic steroids

Anabolic-androgenic steroids are drugs that are related to male hormones. Anabolic steroids are connected to muscle building, and androgenic steroids are connected to increased masculine characteristics. These drugs are available only by prescription. They are prescribed to treat low levels of testosterone, a male hormone. Athletes and other individuals use steroids to improve their performance.

Side effects of illegal use can include liver tumors, jaundice, high blood pressure, and severe acne. Men can experience infertility, development of breasts, shrinking of the testicles, and baldness. Women can experience growth of facial hair, deepened voice, and changes in or stopping of the menstrual cycle.

The chemical name and generic name of anabolic steroids are:
- Anabolin (Nandrolone)
- Durabolin (Nandrolone)
- Anabolin LA-100 (Nandrolone)
- Hybolin Decanoate (Nandrolone Decanoate)
- Android (Methyl Testosterone)
- Hybolin Improved (Nandrolone)
- Anadrol (Oxymetholone)
- Metandren (Methyl Testosterone)
- Anavar (Oxandrolone)
- Oreton (Methyl Testosterone)
- Androlone (Nandrolone)
- Nandrobolic (Nandrolone)
- Androlone 50 (Nandrolone)
- Nandrobolic L.A. (Nandrolone Decanoate)
- Androlone D (Nandrolone Decanoate)
- Neo-Durabolic (Nandrolone)
- Deca-Durabolin (Nandrolone Decanoate)
- Virilon (Methyl Testosterone)

- Winstrol (Stanozolol)

Psychotropics antidepressants

The psychoactive chemicals found in the psychotropics (alters perception and behavior) antidepressants family along with the trade names are:
- Dibenzoxazepine - Amoxapine (Asendin)
- MAOI (Irreversible) - Isocarboxazid (Marplan), Phenelzine (Nardil), Tranylcypromine (Parnate)

Copyright © Mometrix Media. You have been licensed one copy of this document for personal use only. Any other reproduction or redistribution is strictly prohibited. All rights reserved.

- MAOI (RIMA) - Moclobemide (Manerix)
- Monocyclic - Bupropion (Wellbutrin)
- Selective Serotonin Reuptake Inhibitors- Fluoxetine (Prozac), Fluvoxamine (Luvox), Paroxetine (Paxil), Sertraline (Zoloft)
- Selective Norepinephine/Serotonin Reuptake Inhibitors - Effexor (Venlafaxine HCL)
- Tetracyclic - Amitriptyline (Elavil), Colmipramine (Anafranil), Desipramine (Norpramin), Doxepin (Sinequan, Triadapin), Imipramine (Torfanil), Nortriptyline (Aventyl, Pamelor), Protriptyline (Triptil, Vivactil), Trimipramine (Surmontil),
- Triazolopyridine - Trazodone (Desyrel)
- Novel - Serzone (Nefazodone), Wellbutrin, Zyban (Bupropion)

Antipsychotics

The psychoactive chemicals found in the psychotropics antipsychotic family along with their trade names are:
- Aliphatic Phenothiazines - Chlorpromazine (Largactil, Thorazine), Methotrimeprazine (Nozinan, Levoprome), Triflupromazine (Vesprin)
- Benzamide - not available in the U.S. Remoxipride (Roxiam)
- Benzisoxazole - Risperidone (Risperadol)
- Butyrophenone - Haloperidol (Haldol), Haloperidol Decanoate (Haldol LA)
- Dibenzodiazepine - Clozapine (Clozaril)
- Dibenzoxazepine - Loxapine (Loxapac, Loxitane)
- Diphenylbutylpiperidines - Fluspirilene (Imap) not available in the U.S., Pimozide (Orap)

- Dihydroindolone - Molindone (Moban)
- Piperidine Phenothiazines - Mesoridazine (Seerentil), Pericyazine (Neuleptil), Pipotiazine palmitate (Piportil L4), Thioridazine (Mellaril)
- Piperazine Phenothiazines - Acetophenazine (Tindal), Fluphenazine HCL (Moditen, Prolixin), Fluphenazine enanthate (Moditen inj., Prolixin enanthate), Fluphenazine decanoate (Modecate, Prolixin decanoate). Perphenazine (Trilafon), Thioproperazine (Majeptil), Trifluoperazine (Stelazine),
- Atypical - Risperdal (Risperidone), Zyprexa (Olanzapine), Seroqual (Quietapine),
- Thioxanthenes, Chlorprothixene (Taractan), Flupenthixol (Fluanxol), Flupenthixol decanoate (Fluanxol inj.), Thiothixene (Navane)

Mood stabilizers

The psychoactive chemicals found in the psychotropics antipsychotic family and the mood stabilizer family along with their trade names are:
- Anticonvulsants: Carbamazepine (Tegretol), Clonazepam (Klonopin, Rivotril), Lamictal (Lamotrigine), Neurontin (Gabapentin), Valproate (Depakene, Epival)
- Lithium: Lithium (Lithane, Carbolith)

Designer psychoactive chemicals analogue categories

The analogue categories of Fentanyl and Meperidine (Demerol) are inhaled or injected. They provide relief from pain much like the opiates they are made from.

- 23 -

Copyright © Mometrix Media. You have been licensed one copy of this document for personal use only. Any other reproduction or redistribution is strictly prohibited. All rights reserved.

Dangers include drowsiness, depression of the respiratory system, muscle rigidity, impaired speech, paralysis and irreversible brain damage. Ecstasy, known as MDMA, is a hallucinogen but was introduced as an appetite suppressant. It can be made from MDA and methamphetamine. It is also known as the "love drug". Dangers include tight muscles, nausea/vomiting, dehydration, changes in blood sugar, pulse and blood pressure, and hallucinations. MPTP is made from meperidine. It freezes the body and causes the symptoms of Parkinson's disease. MX'ING is combining Ecstasy ("X") and hallucinogenic mushrooms ("Shrooms").

Ecstasy, GHB, Ketamine, and Rohypnol

Club drugs are drugs which teens and young adults use in the nightclub, bar and concert scene. Ecstasy (MDMA) is a synthetic drug in the psychoactive group. It is similar to methamphetamine and mescaline. On the street it is known as Ecstasy, XTC, and hug drug.
Harmful levels in the body can be reached in a very short period of time. GHB and Rohypnol are colorless, tasteless, and odorless depressants to the central nervous system. They are often added to beverages and are not detected by the drinker. Therefore, they are known as "date rape" drugs. Ketamine is an anesthetic, which is injected or snorted. It causes dream-like states and hallucinations.

Talwin and Ritalin

Talwin (pentazocine) and Ritalin (methylphenidate) are mixed and sold on the street. This mixture is known as "Ts and Rs", "Ts and Rits", "One and Ones", and "Set". Talwin and Ritalin are both prescription drugs. Talwin is a painkiller, and Ritalin is a stimulant. When they are combined and injected, the user experiences an intense euphoric high.

This high is very similar to the combination of heroin and cocaine. It is very brief and therefore leads to greater use. Tolerance to the drugs may develop as well as a dependence on both Talwin and Ritalin. When withdrawal occurs, insomnia, abdominal cramping, and nausea may be present as well as a deep depression and exhaustion. The withdrawal symptoms of each drug are compounded because of the combination of the two.

Short and long-term effects
Short-term effects of the mixture of Talwin and Ritalin most often include infections caused by dirty needles. These infections can include skin ulcers, infected veins, and abscesses. Bacterial infections of the lungs, bones, and heart also occur and are very serious. Viral infections of the liver can also occur. Another danger from the shared use of needles is HIV. Dizziness, paranoia, constipation, anorexia, nausea, confusion, and tremors can also be side effects. Increases in blood pressure and hallucinations have been noted in high dose users. Coma and death have been caused by extremely high doses.

Long-term effects may include a toxic psychosis. This psychosis is characterized by hallucinations, delusions and confusion. Another effect may be damage to the lungs by the filler used in the production of both Talwin and Ritalin.

Important terms

- Recreational use - refers to the use of chemicals in a social setting with a group of friends who are all using to get the effects of the drugs. The use is infrequent and usually only small amounts of the drugs are used.
- Circumstantial use - refers to chemical use to get a particular

- 24 -

Copyright © Mometrix Media. You have been licensed one copy of this document for personal use only. Any other reproduction or redistribution is strictly prohibited. All rights reserved.

effect in a particular situation such as truck drivers using stimulants to stay awake when they are driving for long periods of time.

- Compulsive use - refers to use of chemicals on a daily basis. Also, the amount of the chemical taken is large. The purpose in usage is to get a desired effect. This use is the most dangerous and is usually classified as addiction.
- Intensified use - refers to use of chemicals on a daily or almost daily basis, but in low amounts. The purpose of this type of use is to help alleviate some problem or to boost levels of performance.
- Abuse liability - involves the question "what are the chances or odds of a drug causing addiction?"
- Controlled substance - Any drug that has an abuse liability and is placed on restricted use by the DEA.
- Poly-chemical abuse - occurs when more than one psychoactive chemical is used at a time.
- Antagonist - a psychoactive chemical that reverses the effects of another psychoactive chemical. There are narcotic antagonists and benzodiazepine antagonists.
- Schedules I-V - are the groups that psychoactive chemicals are put into according to their abuse liability and usefulness for medical treatment. Schedule I has the chemicals that have no medical use and a high abuse liability. Schedules II - V contain chemicals that are valuable for their medical use but can only be prescribed by a doctor. Schedule V contains the most abuse liability.
- Cross dependence - refers to similar drugs substituting for each other within the body and preventing withdrawal and/or similar drugs preserving the state of dependence
- Dependence - A compulsive pattern of drug use involving getting a supply, extreme involvement in the use, and high relapse occurrences after withdrawal.
- Detoxification - when cross dependent chemicals are substituted for the chemical which is being abused together with a slow withdrawal of that chemical
- Designer psychoactive chemicals - chemicals made in labs from legal drugs that have the same effects as some illegal drugs
- Dual diagnosis - occurs when a patient is diagnosed with a mental illness as well as addiction or abuse of a drug.
- Over-the-counter chemical - drugs that are available without prescriptions.
- Huffing - breathing vapors from a substance in a bag through the nose and mouth.
- Nitrate "poppers" - used to improve sexual performance.
- Butyl/isobutyl - used to improve sexual pleasure - street names: "Locker Room", "Rush", "Bolt", "Quicksilver", "Zoom" and is found in room deodorizers.
- Inhalant laughing gas - nitrous oxide found in dentists' offices, bakeries, and whipped cream aerosol cans and is used as an inhalant.

Copyright © Mometrix Media. You have been licensed one copy of this document for personal use only. Any other reproduction or redistribution is strictly prohibited. All rights reserved.

Theoretical Base of Counseling

REBT

The Rational-Emotive-Behavioral Theory (REBT) is based on the principle that people are not disturbed by events but rather how they see the event. Attitudes and negative self-concepts can start and maintain the process of addiction. REBT concentrates on the here and now rather than the past as to how a person's attitudes, beliefs and self-concepts affect his emotions and behavior. Active, systematic, and directive interventions can correct thoughts that are irrational which cause unhappy lives.

The ABC model of this therapy is as follows:
- A--activating event
- B--beliefs and thoughts
- C--consequences (both emotional and behavioral).

One of the beliefs of this model is that the motivations that cause self-defeating behaviors of chemical addictions are discomfort, anxiety and low frustration tolerance. The counselor's job is to help the patient to replace these behaviors with rational behaviors.

The principle that drives the Rational-Emotive-Behavioral Theory (REBT) is the belief that it is not an actual event that disturbs a person, but rather, how he sees that event:
- Negative life events are labeled A's for Activating Events.
- The B's are the thoughts and beliefs that are felt about the behaviors and emotions surrounding the events. B's are the problem causers.
- C's are the consequences (behaviors and emotions) that result from the negative life events.

When the A-B-C model is applied to addiction, it is believed that discomfort, low tolerance to frustration, and anxiety are the motivators that cause the self-defeating behaviors of addiction. These behaviors result in dysfunctional beliefs like, "Life is very tough so I am entitled to a drink (or drug)." The therapist's job is to get rid of these beliefs by doing things to question the client's faulty thinking. Rational beliefs are suggested to replace the irrational ones.

Behavioral Modification Theory

The Behavioral Modification Theory is based on the idea that all behavior is learned, and what is learned can be unlearned. Three learning processes are tied to the cause, support and change of behavior:
- The first is classical conditioning or substituting a stimulus which brings about the same result. Classical conditioning learning has provided the following types of addiction treatment Procedures: cue exposure, stimulus control, relaxation, and aversion therapy.
- Operant conditioning is based on the increase or decrease of certain behaviors through the use of reinforcement. Negative reinforcement can decrease a behavior. Operant conditioning has provided the treatment style of reinforcing desired behaviors and punishing those that are not desirable.
- The final process is called modeling. This means learning a behavior by observing another performing the behavior. Then a

Copyright © Mometrix Media. You have been licensed one copy of this document for personal use only. Any other reproduction or redistribution is strictly prohibited. All rights reserved.

practice of the behavior occurs followed by reinforcement.

Classical conditioning has contributed to the following treatment procedures for addiction: cue exposure treatments, stimulus control, relaxation training, and aversion therapy.

Control Theory/Reality Theory

Control Theory/Reality Theory is an approach to counseling which has its base on the idea that it is not the real world that affects one's behavior. Rather, it is how the world is perceived to be. Another principle of CT/RT is that people do not have to be a victim of what has happened in the past unless they let it. There are four parts to CT/RT: doing, thinking, feeling and physiology. This means that one may not have the ability to change the way his body functions or his feelings, but he does have the power to change the ways he acts and thinks. Another underlying principle is the emphasis on taking responsibility for satisfying one's needs without interfering with the needs of others. A focus is on a client changing his total behavior not just his attitudes and feelings. Changing feelings or physiology is very difficult, but changing what one does or how one thinks is completely within reason. The way one acts is directly related to satisfying needs. CT/RT believes that individuals choose negative reactions to external events even though they may be harmful because they serve a purpose. CT/RT is based on the principle of individuals having a success identity. In so doing, they have feelings of self-worth which provide strength. The emphasis of CT/RT is on the responsibility of taking control of one's own life. Techniques of counseling should focus on the giving of direction, current behavior evaluation, and then making a plan and committing to it.

Person-Centered Therapy

Person-Centered Therapy is made up of provisional ideas. One of these ideas is that it is the patient's responsibility to find ways to deal with reality. The counselor's job is to try to understand how the patient sees himself as well as the world. An accepting, genuine and empathetic counselor may be able to bring this about. This type of therapy can decrease the defensiveness of the patient as well as to help them see themselves as they really are. It also produces a safe atmosphere in which the patient can take risks in promoting change. They can also look into their inner selves to find answers regarding many issues. The patient's acceptance of himself may be fostered by the acceptance of the counselor. Person-Centered Therapy was not designed to be a one method only of treatment. Neither is it a dogma. Instead it is considered to be an uncertain set of ideas that center on the idea that it is the patient's responsibility to find ways to deal with reality. When an individual knows himself well then he will be able to identify his best behavior. In so doing, he becomes more aware of himself. One of the principles of this therapy is for the counselor to try to come to an understanding of how the patient sees himself and the rest of the world. The principle has three elements.

- One is referred to as congruence or the demonstration of being real and genuine.
- Next is positive regard meaning being accepting and caring.
- Finally, empathy, which is the ability to see the world from the viewpoint of the patient, needs to be demonstrated. A clear understanding of the patient should be shown.

Copyright © Mometrix Media. You have been licensed one copy of this document for personal use only. Any other reproduction or redistribution is strictly prohibited. All rights reserved.

Freudian or Psychoanalytical Therapy

Freudian or Psychoanalytical Therapy is based on the idea that people are influenced considerably by their unconscious, inner drives. Conflict is caused by three systems interacting. The source of unconscious drives is called the id. The internalized outside world is called the superego. Anxiety is created when there is conflict between the id and the superego. The third system, the ego, takes the force of the conflict. This results in the creation of defense mechanisms such as denial. This therapy is helpful in situations where there are many relapses and serious personality disturbances. Getting rid of defense mechanisms can help the patient to feel less threatened. This insecurity has led to abuse in the past. The therapy can also identify the source of many cravings leading to the abuse. An additional principle is that all persons go through five stages of life - oral, anal, phallic, latency, and genital. However, sometimes a person gets stuck in one stage which causes problems.

Adlerian or Individual Therapy

Adlerian or Individual Therapy was developed by Adler who believed that social urges were what influenced people. It was based on the idea that people are always striving to be better or perfect. When these levels are not reached, a feeling of inferiority is felt and dissatisfaction is present. This model of counseling is often thought of as a growth model. Behavior is believed to have a purpose. A term that refers to everyone having a goal that provides a purpose is fictional finalism. Sometimes fictional finalism can be negative and lead to chemical abuse. Some concepts which influence this theory are the belief of social interest which has to do with a person's concepts about being a part of the human community. Identification of faulty goals and assumptions is helpful for addiction counseling. It also helps patients to be able to feel better about themselves and to feel less discouraged. One of the principles upon which Adlerian or Individual Therapy is based is the fact that therapists who use this model try to see the world from the viewpoint of their patient. A second principle is the belief that there is a purpose for all behavior. Another viewpoint of Adlerian Therapy is the belief that there is an imaginary goal, fictional finalism, that directs all human behavior and gives humans a purpose. Sometimes this fictional finalism can result in negative behaviors. The next principle is called social interest and refers to the belief that individuals know that they are a part of the world community. This also has to do with how they identify and empathize with others. The last principle is the belief that birth order affects a person's behavior.

Gestalt Therapy

Gestalt Therapy is based on the idea that people must accept responsibility for what happens to them and to find their own way in life. One very important principle in therapy is to help the patient to discover what they want to be rather than trying to be someone else. An important element in treatment is to get the patient to "reown" himself. Gestalt only deals with the present. Therefore this is where change must take place–not the past or future. Contact must be present for change to take place. Contact is in the form of seeing, hearing, smelling, touching, and moving. This therapy stresses living with one's feelings rather than running away, even if those feelings make one feel uncomfortable. This involves taking care of all unfinished business such as dealing with feelings of anger, etc. that have not been expressed. These feelings just remain in a person's life and can gradually lead to the problem of addiction. Patients are encouraged to ask for help when they feel a need.

Copyright © Mometrix Media. You have been licensed one copy of this document for personal use only. Any other reproduction or redistribution is strictly prohibited. All rights reserved.

Accepting responsibility as well as the consequences of behavior is also a part of Gestalt Therapy.

Solution-Focused Therapy

Solution-Focused Therapy is focused on things that work rather than problems. No treatment plans are imposed on the patient. The idea is to work with the beliefs of the patient to promote change. Successes of the patient are the focuses of treatment. Solution-Focused Therapy basis is the belief that the successes of a patient should be dealt with rather than the disabilities or deficits. Using these successes should bring about change. The counselor uses a method called utilization, which uses the good things about the patient to bring about change. The therapist addresses the complaint of the patient by trying to help him to find a solution for that specific complaint. It uses simple and straight-forward methods. What is going to happen in the present as well as the future are the focuses of treatment. The mind-set of Solution-Focused Therapy is when the patient recovers, not if the patient recovers. This is a very positive form of therapy. In addition, it is self-affirming for the patient. A therapist does not confront the patient. Rather, he cooperates with him. Some of the cliches that mirror the principles of this therapy model are: "If it ain't broke, don't fix it."; "Once you know what to do, do more of it."; and "If it doesn't work, do something different." The therapy does not last long so it does not cost a lot. Denial and resistance are just skipped because the end result is expected to be change. Patients from all cultures, stages of addiction, and socio-economic backgrounds are successful.

Pharmacotherapies

Pharmacotherapies means using prescription drugs along with some form of therapy to treat substance abuse. Research is showing that the use of pharmacotherapies is very successful. Some medications which are called sensitizers cause a very unpleasant effect if used in conjunction with the substance which is being abused. Antabuse (disulfiram) is a sensitizer used in the treatment of alcohol abuse. Other medications act as neural blockers (antagonists) which block the effects of the abused drug. An example is Naltrexone which blocks the effects of opiates. Another form of pharmacotherapy is the use of certain drugs to help decrease the extreme withdrawal effects. Benzodiazepines and anti-seizure medicines are aids for this. Some drugs are used to decrease the cravings caused by some substances. Methadone has been shown to be successful in the treatment of heroin abuse. Also anti-depressants and anti-psychotics have their place in treatment of persons who have mental disorders too.

The principles upon which the use of pharmacotherapies is based are:

- Prescription drugs can be used to detox, stabilize, and maintain individuals with substance abuse.
- They can also be used as antagonists and to treat other co-existing medical problems.
- Some drugs can be used as sensitizers which cause unpleasant conditions in the body if certain drugs are taken while the sensitizer is in the system. An example is Antabuse which reacts with alcohol.
- Other drugs act as blockers (antagonists). They block the effects of certain drugs while in the system. An example is Naltrexone which blocks the effects of opiates.

Copyright © Mometrix Media. You have been licensed one copy of this document for personal use only. Any other reproduction or redistribution is strictly prohibited. All rights reserved.

- Some drugs are used to help alleviate dangerous withdrawal symptoms. Examples are benzodiazepines and anti-seizure medications.
- Cravings can be decreased during recovery by the use of certain drugs.

Motivational Enhancement Therapy

The basis of Motivational Enhancement Therapy is motivational psychology. It is a very systematic form of treatment that should cause a change in individuals with drinking problems. Change is internally motivated and is very rapid because it is based on the belief that the patient has the capability as well as the responsibility to change. The therapist's job is to motivate and mobilize the conditions that enhance the commitment to changes. The therapist does not assume an authoritarian position. There is a de-emphasis on labels such as "alcoholic". There is an emphasis on personal choices regarding drug use together with an objective evaluation of behavior. Change occurs in the following steps:
- Pre-contemplation (change has not been considered)
- Contemplation (thoughts begin to occur about the possibility of change together with what the costs will be)
- Determination (a decision is made to change)
- Action (behaviors are changed)
- Maintenance (things that made the change possible need to be maintained).

Family Systems and Addiction Counseling

Family Systems and Addiction Counseling is based on the premise that when a person abuses drugs, the whole family is affected. Several models of therapy are being used:
- Dynamic Family Therapy--therapy is based on gaining insight to be able to understand conflicts which are present in the family setting.
- Experiential/Humanistic Family Therapy--therapy is based on the present and the most important factor of recovery is self-determination and self-awareness.
- Bowenian Family Therapy--is based on the concept that emotions and intellect of a family are entangled or fused. This causes an automatic emotional arousal within the family. The other basis is referred to as differentiation where the individual remains without outside control.
- Structural Family Therapy - the counselor tries to change the dysfunctional structure of the family.
- Family Disease Model--based on the idea that alcoholism is a family disease, and the disease itself is codependence.

Twelve Steps of Alcoholics Anonymous

The Twelve Steps of Alcoholics Anonymous are a form of intervention approach:
- Powerless over alcohol--lives are not manageable
- Power greater than ourselves can restore our sanity
- Make a decision to turn things over to God
- Make a thorough moral inventory
- Admission of wrong to self, another, and to God
- Ready to get rid of character defects
- Ask God to remove shortcomings

Copyright © Mometrix Media. You have been licensed one copy of this document for personal use only. Any other reproduction or redistribution is strictly prohibited. All rights reserved.

- Make a list of people hurt and become willing to make amends
- Make amends to people on list
- Continue to make personal inventories and admit wrongs
- Pray for knowledge of God's will and power to carry it out
- Try to carry the message to others and to practice all these steps

Taxonomy of pathology

Taxonomy of pathology is the classification of problems into two groups called Axis I disorders which include behavioral disorders as well as some physical disorders and Axis II disorders which are only behavioral. Originally, Axis I had about 60 different disorders. There were no sharp distinctions between normal and abnormal. The thought was that everyone is a little abnormal. People who were severe had more trouble functioning. Also there were two large categories in Axis I: psychosis and neurosis. The psychosis category had severe mental disorders, and the neurosis category was categorized by distortions in reality such as depression and or anxiety. Now the Axis I category has the major mental disorders, developmental disorders and learning disabilities. The Axis II category has the personality disorders and mental retardation.

Substance abuse and domestic violence

A link between substance abuse and domestic violence has been established. The following data gives evidence to that link:
- Children from homes that have violence have indicated that their fathers had a drinking problem and were more likely to abuse family members when drinking.

- Substance abuse by youth has been connected to physical abuse suffered as a child.
- Recovering women are seen to have a history of violence.
- Women who are alcoholics have a higher frequency of physical and emotional abuse during childhood.
- Half of the persons who batter others have had substance abuse problems.
- Half of the persons who have murdered their spouses had been drinking.
- Three times more children have been reported to protective services who come from homes in which there is substance abuse.
- The probability of a parent being able to protect a child decreases when the other parent is a substance abuser.

Effects of battering and victimization on treatment
Battering and victimization affect treatment of substance abuse in both direct and indirect ways:
- Violence on the part of the spouse toward a woman in treatment occurs frequently. The spouse may feel threatened when treatment is being sought, and then he becomes angry which leads to violence or threats.
- Also, some women in treatment are bullied into using substances with the spouse.
- Further instances that cause a roadblock occur when the spouse gets the woman in treatment to make up with him after violence occurs by using alcohol or other drugs with him.
- Threats of violence, holding back money, and abuse of the children are also used by the violent spouse.

Copyright © Mometrix Media. You have been licensed one copy of this document for personal use only.
Any other reproduction or redistribution is strictly prohibited. All rights reserved.

- On the other hand, many individuals who batter their spouses are nicer when they are using drugs. Therefore, sobriety is not a desired result on the part of the spouse who is getting battered.

Conflict between abuse and domestic violence treatment

Many times substance abuse treatment and domestic violence programs appear to be in conflict. It is often an either/or situation because the safety factor for a woman must be taken into consideration before a treatment program for her substance abuse can take place. A spouse many times will remain in the violent home because the batterer is the supplier of the drugs. So, which problem is to be solved remains to be decided on a case to case basis. Priority determines what is treated first. Differences in the terminology that is used in the two programs is another conflicting factor. Often terms such as denial, codependency, and powerlessness are seen as stigmatizing and self-defeating in helping individuals who are in violence abuse situations as well as substance abuse treatment. There are more males in treatment programs, which causes a female who is a victim of violence to feel that the treatment is irrelevant.

Adolescent physical, mental, personality and social development

The characteristics of adolescent physical development:
- Primary sex characteristics -sex organs mature
- Secondary sex characteristics-development of breasts and facial hair appear
- Genital development and facial hair directed by t male hormones, testosterone

- Genital and breast development directed by female hormones, estrogen and progesterone
- Females begin menstruation

The characteristics of adolescent mental development:
- Immature mental operations left behind
- Rational thinking develops
- Thinking becomes more flexible and abstract
- Deductive reasoning used in problem solving
- Inductive reasoning used in problem solving
- Self-centeredness is present - concerned with what people think about them

The characteristics of adolescent personality and social development:
- Identify is formed - distinctive person emerges
- Identity vs. role diffusion
- Identify achievement - goals and values are committed to
- Identify diffusion - goals and values not examined
- Identity foreclosure - others set goals
- Identity moratorium - no commitment goal
- Individuation -separation of attitudes and beliefs from those of parents

Development of young adulthood

Characteristics of physical development:
- Physical growth and maturation has ended
- Complete muscle growth
- Physical potential has been reached
- Maximum brain size and weight
- Little change in sense modalities

Copyright © Mometrix Media. You have been licensed one copy of this document for personal use only. Any other reproduction or redistribution is strictly prohibited. All rights reserved.

Characteristics of mental development:
- Maximum capacity to acquire and utilize knowledge
- Problem solving is systematic and sophisticated
- Qualitative and quantitative dimensions reached

Characteristics of personality and social change:
- Ability to develop an intimate relationship
- Mutual trust is the basis for an intimate relationship
- Development of interdependence
- Development of communication which is effective
- Sensitive to others
- Ability to live in an adult world is developed
- Not as dependent on family
- Time of intimacy vs. isolation

Development of late adulthood

Physical characteristics:
- Osteoporosis and arthritis
- Eye problems
- Wrinkling of skin
- Graying/thinning hair
- Less effective immune system
- Changes in urinary and gastrointestinal systems
- Concerns with dental
- Decreases in brain weight and size
- Respiratory system less productive
- Heart tissue may atrophy
- Decrease in musculoskeletal system

Mental characteristics:
- Memory changes
- Alzheimer's
- Dementia

Personality and Social characteristics:
- Time of integrity vs. despair

- Institutionalized care
- Awareness of aging and end of life
- Struggle with discrimination
- Dignified retirement with security
- Consolidated personality

Important terms

- Puberty - the stage of development during adolescence when reproductive organs and sex characteristics such as breasts and facial hair appear.
- Testosterone - the male sex hormones that affect the development of genitals and hair on the face.
- Estrogen and progesterone - the female sex hormones that affect the development of genitals and breasts.
- Menarche - the time when a female's menstrual period begins.
- Deductive reasoning - the ability to solve problems by working from a given situation to a conclusion.
- Inductive reasoning - the ability to solve problems by working from a specific experience to a conclusion.
- Adolescent egocentrism - self-centeredness based on the concern about what others think.
- Identity formation - process that a person goes through in becoming a distinctive individual.
- Identity achievement - occurs when a person sets a goal based on his values.

Copyright © Mometrix Media. You have been licensed one copy of this document for personal use only. Any other reproduction or redistribution is strictly prohibited. All rights reserved.

Counseling Practice

Addiction counselor

Education, support and nonjudgmental confrontation make up the role of the addiction counselor. A good relationship with the patient is extremely important. The patient needs to feel like the counselor understands his problems and is on his side. The counselor acts as a guide for the patient during the early stages of recovery, but the patient must eventually take responsibility for the outcome. If confrontation must occur, the counselor should show a supportive attitude rather than a judgmental one. Balance needs to be found between respect for the patient, where he is, and where he is going coupled with the problems involved and a need to direct and exert pressure if needed to point him in the direction of recovery and abstinence. It is important to realize when to direct and when to let the patient be self-directed. This process can be made easier if the counselor has a structured session.

Counseling

Counseling is regular management of patients who are addicted through support, encouragement, provision of structure, observation of behavior, provision of other services, and referrals for employment counseling and medical and legal services. Types of counseling include individual, group, and family. Settings for counseling include detox centers, public and private clinics, residential treatment centers, hospitals, penal institutions, day treatment centers, community centers, halfway houses, methadone maintenance programs, and several others.

Therapeutic alliance

A sense of partnership and collaboration must be established by the Counselor:
- First, the counselor must have a broad knowledge of addiction and how addicts live.
- Second, the counselor has to express that nobody knows better than the addict about his own life
- Third, the counselor must get across the fact that he is an ally in this battle for recovery.

The counselor must be a good listener, be able to convey empathy, and avoid being judgmental. Luborsky et al. 1997 proposes that the interventions that are the most effective in molding a strong therapeutic alliance are active listening on the part of the counselor and development of a sense of collaboration between the counselor and the patient. The counselor should be willing to let the patient express his opinion about problems that may be present in the treatment session.

Appropriate behavior

First, the counselor should not be hard and judgmental in discussing the addiction. He should not blame the patient for having the behaviors for causing the addiction. Addicts already feel a great deal of shame and guilt because of their addiction. They should be encouraged to feel free to talk honestly about their behaviors and to know that what they say will be accepted. Next, a feeling of respect must be present. No derogatory and disrespectful comments should occur. The counselor should be on time and professional in his manner. It is not a good idea to share one's own personal experiences unless there is a plan in place in which self-disclosure would serve a good purpose such as

Copyright © Mometrix Media. You have been licensed one copy of this document for personal use only. Any other reproduction or redistribution is strictly prohibited. All rights reserved.

getting the patient to open up or to provide a role model.

Successful counseling program

The following components are all parts of a successful counseling program:

- Deals with the client's immediate needs such as food
- Encourages and supports efforts to reduce substance abuse
- Monitors progress as defined by the treatment progress plan
- Provides medical connections
- Gets legal advice
- Keeps accurate records
- Enforces treatment program rules which encourages the setting of limits
- Provides coordination of services
- Uses structured format
- Provides specific education which is geared toward each individual client
- Recommends using self-help groups such as AA
- Encourages good physical health
- Includes family members in treatment
- Maintains current knowledge regarding abused drugs including pharmacology, how administered, patterns of use, drug combinations, adverse effects, research, and his client's preferred drug
- Maintains good relationship with other professionals

Counselor/client relationship

The relationship between client and counselor is the basis for all of the rest of the treatment program. Both parties are responsible for its creation. Key parts are the combination of:

- Agreement on goals
- Client-counselor bond
- Cooperation between parties

Other elements which help to create a good relationship include:

- Understanding on the part of the counselor as to where the client is coming from
- A cultural understanding by the counselor
- A demonstration by the counselor that he wants to understand
- Paying attention to what is important to the client.
- It is also important for the counselor to be genuine, warm, and consistent in word and deed. It is important for the counselor to share what is happening immediately and to be able to stay focused.
- Respect for the client shows that the counselor is committed to understanding and helping in a non-judgmental, warm atmosphere.

Self-disclosure by the counselor

Self-disclosure can help to establish a warm, empathetic atmosphere. It often can help the client to not feel alone and promote his own disclosure. It can be used for role-modeling as well as to develop new perceptions for the client. Before using self-disclosure the counselor should look at the benefits for the client. Anything disclosed should relate directly to the client's situation. The best rule is to not disclose a large amount of information. Too much can restrict the client's input, make him feel that the counselor has problems and is not trustworthy. If disclosure comes too early in the treatment process, it can cause feelings of inferiority and rejection on the part of the client. It can also cause the client to have feelings of anxiety. Do not use self-disclosure if it might burden the client. Therefore, a certain amount of risk is possible by using self-disclosure.

Copyright © Mometrix Media. You have been licensed one copy of this document for personal use only. Any other reproduction or redistribution is strictly prohibited. All rights reserved.

Client evaluation

Screening process

The primary goal of screening is to determine if the client is right for a facility. It is a process of ruling out. The establishment of rapport is very helpful at this stage because it helps the client to provide a more accurate picture. An essential element of screening is the collection of basic information about the client such as name, address, age, etc. Another element is the explanation of confidentiality guidelines and limitations. Next, an overview of the program itself should be provided which would include what is covered, cost, how to schedule appointments, the philosophy or goals of the program, and a description or explanation about the credentials of the service providers. Another element of the screening process is the use of certain tests which are preliminary assessment instruments.

Assessment process

If the client is determined to be right for the program during the screening process, then the next step is to make an accurate and broad-scoped assessment. The objectives of the assessment are:

- To identify someone who has a problem with addiction
- To assess other problems that may be present
- To plan interventions
- To involve family members in the assessment and treatment
- To plan methods to test the effectiveness of the interventions.

The assessment begins with a formal intake process. Then a thorough interview to gather information ranging from basics, family history, education, employment, cultural background, religious/spiritual background, legal issues, psychosexual history, issues of abuse, history of social skills, general development, and a drug and alcohol history. Information about co-existing mental health issues, mental status exam, and previous treatment are also gathered. A final Assessment Guide is formulated followed by a Clinical Summation.

Treatment planning process

The treatment plan needs to reflect the most important points discovered in the assessment. The plan should explain the findings of the assessment.

- It should interpret all of the data reported.
- Also, the readiness of the client to take part in treatment should be determined.
- The priority of problems and needs should be established.
- A statement of needs should be made by both the client and counselor.
- Then a statement of how the needs can be met should be made.
- An identification of the various interventions should be executed.
- Coordination of treatment activities with the client's diagnosis should be made then.

The treatment plan can be in many forms but should include:

- A problem statement
- A goal statement
- A list of measurable objectives, and
- The particular strategies that will be used.

A treatment plan should be realistic and designed for the individual.

Referral process

The referral process has eight elements and is used to determine if other community resources and support systems are needed in the treatment of a client. The elements are as follows:

Copyright © Mometrix Media. You have been licensed one copy of this document for personal use only. Any other reproduction or redistribution is strictly prohibited. All rights reserved.

- A relationship should be established with other agencies, community groups, and professionals
- Continual re-evaluation and assessment of sources to find out how appropriate they are
- Be able to determine the difference between a situation where the client can refer himself and when the counselor should refer
- Meet the client's needs by referring him to other agencies, programs or professionals
- Be able to make a clear explanation to the client about why he or she needs the referral
- Exchange information which is important to the treatment with the referral agency
- Be aware of the importance of confidentiality
- Determine the effectiveness of the referral

Service coordination

Service coordination is the process in which the client, outside agencies, outside resources, and treatment program are brought together in order to meet the needs identified in the treatment plan. This process combines the administrative, evaluative, and clinical components. Certain elements of service coordination must be present:

- First, the treatment plan has to be implemented.
- Next there must be a working together with the source of referral.
- All of the data from the screening, assessment, and treatment planning must be reviewed and interpreted.
- A decision must be made regarding whether the client is

eligible for admission and ready for the treatment.
- Paperwork and any other procedures for admission must be completed.
- Finally the expectations of the individualized treatment must be established and the family members informed.

Continuing assessment and treatment planning

The counselor needs to continue to play an active role after the admission of the client.

- Continued contact with the client as well as his or her family needs to take place in order to make sure that the treatment plan is in place and is being carried out.
- Also, the counselor needs to be tuned in to any indications of change. He needs to be able to implement change in the plan if necessary.
- Documentation of the process, progress and service coordination is very important.
- A knowledge of and ability to use various tools to measure the effectiveness of the plan is a key component.
- Finally, the counselor should have a knowledge of criteria regarding placement, continued stay and discharge in each stage of the treatment.

Counseling session

The first part of a counseling session should include inquiry by the counselor as to how things are going for the patient and whether or not he or she has had any drug use. If the patient has used drugs, then a discussion of why this relapse took place needs to occur. The discussion should include various ways to keep a

Copyright © Mometrix Media. You have been licensed one copy of this document for personal use only. Any other reproduction or redistribution is strictly prohibited. All rights reserved.

relapse from happening again. If the patient is having personal problems which are directly related to the addiction, then these personal problems should be dealt with before going on. The next stage of the session should include feedback from the counselor about the results of the last drug screen. If the screen was positive for drug use and the patient strongly denies use, then the matter should be dropped for that session. Finally, the patient and counselor should discuss whatever topics are most relevant to the patient's recovery and treatment.

Individual Drug Counseling

The goals and objectives of Individual Drug Counseling are:
- Help the patient to develop better problem-solving strategies.
- Help the patient to recognize and change things that could cause relapse.
- Help the patient to admit that he or she has an addiction problem.
- Help by teaching the patient ways to recognize and redirect urges to use drugs.
- Help the patient to develop better self-esteem by practicing new coping skills.
- Help the patient to realize that using drugs to cope with problems does not work.
- Encourage abstinence. Motivate the patient to abstain from drug use
- Teach the patient that he or she is totally responsible for drug use.
- Introduce the 12 step program. Encourage participation in AA, etc.
- Help the patient to understand that recovery is a life-long process.
- Monitor abstinence by tests such as urinalysis.

- Show the patient the signs and symptoms related to his drug use.

Stage Theory of Addiction model

There are four parts to the Stage Theory of Addiction model:
- Treatment Initiation
- Early Abstinence
- Maintenance of Abstinence
- Advanced Recovery

Patients go through these stages at individual rates. There is overlapping of stages as well as regression sometimes. It is useful to be able to compare this model to where the patient perceives his treatment to be. A patient's needs change as he or she goes through the stages of treatment. A counselor must understand that treatment should be progressive based on these needs. To make sure that the treatment is progressive, the counselor needs to try different methods of intervention, deal with different topics related to recovery, and hold the patient responsible at different levels throughout recovery.

Treatment initiation

The counselor's first job is to get the addict to participate in treatment and to let abstinence become a goal. Many addicts do not want to give up drugs so the counselor must encourage them to discuss these negative feelings. Also the counselor must point out the damage that drug addiction does, bring the denial of being an addict out into the light, and motivate the addict toward recovery. Introduction of the treatment, getting a drug usage history, and developing a plan with the patient are the first steps. The counselor must establish rapport with the patient. An understanding of the expectations and goals of the program by the patient is critical. He or she must also understand that the problem being

Copyright © Mometrix Media. You have been licensed one copy of this document for personal use only. Any other reproduction or redistribution is strictly prohibited. All rights reserved.

addressed is the drug addiction and be willing to work toward recovery.

Denial and ambivalence

Denial is defined as the refusal to accept something in one's life as being real. An addict might refuse to believe that he or she is addicted to drugs. Often, they believe that the problem can be fixed by just cutting down. Addicts also do not believe there is any connection between their main drug usage and any secondary drugs. Many times an addict does not believe that AA or similar organizations can be helpful because they are not like the other people who attend. Ambivalence is the feeling of contradictory emotions or feelings at the same time for an object or person. An example is love and hate for the same person. Addicts often enter treatment with feelings of ambivalence regarding staying sober. They may hate what the addiction does to them but are unable to see life without that drug use.

Maintaining abstinence

The stage known as "maintaining abstinence" occurs when the addict has achieved abstinence. He or she now can recognize the triggers (environmental, emotional, and psychosocial) that cause the drug use. The addict is also developing healthy coping skills for the stresses of life. The most important thing to address during this stage is the danger of relapse. Being honest about feelings and attending self-help groups are both good things for the addict to do. The role of the counselor during this stage is to help the patient to maintain abstinence. Encouragement, teaching, assisting, and helping are ways that the counselor can help to achieve the goals. During this stage the patient is practicing the "drug-free" lifestyle. He or she must keep a humble attitude toward their addiction and not take the abstinence for granted.

Relapse

The steps identified by Gorski and Miller that will hasten a patient into relapse are as follows:
- The patient shows a change in attitude related to his view of the importance of taking part in the recovery program.
- The patient overreacts to stressful events in his life.
- The patient is unwilling to talk about the stressors in his life or even denies their existence.
- Withdrawal symptoms of the patient reappear.
- A change in the daily routine of the patient occurs such as sleeping late or not eating.
- A change in behaviors or attitudes of the patient appears.
- The patient's social interactions change such as withdrawal from friends and family.
- Difficulty in making wise choices is present. The patient may overreact or be apathetic.
- Difficulty in making decisions and judgments is demonstrated by the patient.
- The patient feels stressed and feels that there is no alternative other than drug use.
- Finally, drug use is resumed.

Skills to prevent relapse

Being able to recognize when one is headed for a relapse is a valuable preventive skill. Those danger signals are negative changes in attitudes, feelings and behaviors. The addict must develop the skill to deal with these feelings without using drugs. The counselor can teach the addict how to recognize these signals. Then the addict needs to be taught how to intervene and change these feelings and behaviors. A plan should be developed that includes concrete behavioral changes

Copyright © Mometrix Media. You have been licensed one copy of this document for personal use only. Any other reproduction or redistribution is strictly prohibited. All rights reserved.

that will need to be made in order for the patient to be successful. More frequent attendance at meetings of AA or similar groups, avoiding environmental triggers, putting more structure into their lives, and spending more time with people who are supportive of their recovery are behavioral changes which will be helpful in preventing relapse.

Assessment of relapse

Many factors need to be considered when assessing relapse:
- Do not try to frighten the client.
- Work with the client to set up treatment plans in which both parties are in agreement.
- Minimize confrontations.
- Make sure that the client understands the meanings of labels before forcing him to accept them.
- Look at the history of the family which should include any patterns of relapse. Then look at the client's history of relapse especially any changes in patterns.
- Target the emotional factors that might have been involved.
- Take a look at the client's self-help history and any substitute addictions.
- Examine the strength and intensity of any external or internal relapse triggers.
- Determine if there is a biological risk.

The use of relapse -oriented testing is a valuable tool. Some examples are the Inventory of Drinking Situations and the Situational Confidence Questionnaire.

Relapse treatment

Some considerations for relapse treatment are:

- Stabilize the client.
- Use detox if necessary.
- Help the client understand that relapse is a process as well as an event.
- Help the client to be aware of the chemical cues as well as the cravings.
- Help the client to identify triggers that are high risk and to develop strategies to offset them.
- Get the client involved in assertiveness training.
- Help the client to learn problem-solving skills.
- Show the importance of an exercise program.
- Introduce the skill of meditation.
- Teach how to refuse.
- Teach how to develop other activities.
- Help the client to set up a support network.
- Help the client to develop a means of dealing with negative thoughts.
- Get the family members involved in treatment.
- Help the client to implement a relapse plan.
- Implement the use of preventive tools.
- Encourage the use of a sponsor.

Relapse risk factors

Relapse of an addict can happen at any time in the recovery process. If the addict is aware of situations and problems which can trigger the relapse, he is armed with a tool to perhaps prevent this relapse.
- Warning signs such as changes in feelings, behavior and attitudes should be red flags that a relapse might be eminent.
- Holding in anger or lack of healthy anger management are possible problems.

Copyright © Mometrix Media. You have been licensed one copy of this document for personal use only. Any other reproduction or redistribution is strictly prohibited. All rights reserved.

- Feelings of guilt which do not go away, extreme fatigue, expressions of denial, and unreasonable fears can all be triggers for relapse.
- In addition, feelings of helplessness, boredom, depression, anxiety, and nervousness are also problems that may lead to relapse.

Coping strategies need to be developed to deal with the cravings that occur during recovery. Some coping strategies include:
- Talking the feelings out with someone,
- Changing the activity in which a risk factor seems to be present,
- Changing one's risky attitudes.

Myths surrounding relapse

Some of the myths surrounding relapse include:
- Relapse is not predictable.
- The first act of using a substance is the beginning of relapse.
- Lack of willpower is the cause of relapse.
- Relapse is a conscious decision on the part of the addict.
- Relapse can only occur if the drug which was used to begin with is used again.
- Hitting bottom is the only road to recovery.
- Relapse carries a meaning of failure.
- The client is not motivated; therefore relapse occurs.
- Everyone has the same potential for relapse.
- Negative events are the causes of relapse.
- Relapse crosses out any progress that has been made.
- Withdrawal is completely over in a few days.

- Counselors are not able to predict relapse.

Recovery/Relapse Grid

Relapse-prone style
Individuals in recovery often get to stuck points during recovery. One road that is taken is denial and evasion. The denial and evasion road is called the relapse-prone style.
- Individuals who are prone to relapse deny that recovery is not progressing, avoid other people, and evade or deny problems which occur.
- High-risk factors of this group are poor health maintenance, other illnesses, and high-risk personality or lifestyle.
- Events which can trigger relapse are painful memories and emotions and situations, interactions with persons, or thoughts which are stressful.
- Indicators of internal dysfunction are denial, memory loss, insomnia, and emotional management.
- Indicators of external dysfunction are confusion, depression, avoidance of problems, and behavior that is defensive.
- When loss of control occurs, one will see collapse which is physical or mental, destructive impulses, and poor judgment.
- Signs of the lapse or relapse are loss of the ability to control use, severe shame and guilt, and development of other problems.

Recovery-prone style
Another road which may be taken when an individual gets to a stuck point in recovery is called the recovery-prone style. The individual realizes that a problem does exist, but asks for help and responds appropriately.

Copyright © Mometrix Media. You have been licensed one copy of this document for personal use only. Any other reproduction or redistribution is strictly prohibited. All rights reserved.

- The first stage of this style is transition during which normal problem solving and controlled use strategies fail. A need for abstinence is accepted.
- The next stage is stabilization. The recognition that help is needed and recovery from withdrawal take place. Hope and motivation are developed.
- Early recovery is stage three during which there is a complete consciousness and acceptance of the disease of addiction. Coping skills are learned.
- Middle recovery occurs next. Lifestyle balance is established as well as a self-regulated recovery program.
- Late recovery is characterized by a change of lifestyle and the recognition of the affects of childhood problems on sobriety.
- The final stage is maintenance during which a recovery program is maintained, growth is continued, and coping skills are effective.

Codependency and enabling behavior

Codependency is a condition where another individual such as a spouse or family member is controlled by the addictive behavior of the addict. Acceptance, security, love, and approval all hinge on behaving in the way that the addict wants. This excessive "mothering" only causes more dependency of the addict. Adult children often become codependents because they grew up with the addiction in the home environment.

Enabling behavior occurs when another individual such as a codependent encourages the addict to continue drug use. This behavior can occur both directly or indirectly. An example of this type of behavior might be the lying of a spouse regarding the addiction or the giving of money to the addict so that he or she can buy drugs. It can even be manifest in the covering up of the addiction of a spouse to protect the children.

Spirituality

Spirituality is important in a successful recovery program. It is also known as "healing the self" and is part of the 12 step process. It does not mean a specific religious action, but rather just having values and altruistic goals in life. Patients are encouraged to believe in a higher power than themselves. The higher power goes further than dealing with the daily problems surrounding living. Patients are encouraged to do volunteer service and to participate in the 12 step meetings. Other ways to extend spirituality in their lives might include becoming more involved in religious groups or activities, involvement in community affairs such as animal rescue, and/or involvement in charity work such as walks to support cancer research. Finding happiness and fulfillment by reaching beyond one's self is the central part of the 12 step process. The counselor's job is to introduce and encourage spirituality to the addict.

Shame and guilt

Self-esteem of addicts is severely damaged by feelings of guilt and shame. The negative feeling of shame refers to what the addict believes about himself. Guilt has to do with the belief that the addict has done something wrong. Shame has to do with the person. Guilt has to do with the behavior. The feeling of shame is much more harmful and more difficult to heal. Addicts have both feelings of shame and guilt. They may not feel like they are deserving of recovery. They feel guilt over things they did such as stealing money to buy drugs. Continuing the use of drugs may seem the only way to escape

Copyright © Mometrix Media. You have been licensed one copy of this document for personal use only. Any other reproduction or redistribution is strictly prohibited. All rights reserved.

the pain of shame and guilt. The addict should be encouraged to talk about these feelings. Responsible living should be pointed out as the way to eventually get rid of the painful feelings.

Personal inventory

Taking a personal inventory is a way for an addict to see what he has been through and how he wants his life to be in the future...in other words, where he has been and where he is going. Complete truthfulness and thoroughness is critical to the usefulness. The process can create greater responsibility to oneself and others as well as greater self-acceptance. Personal inventories can be taken repeatedly during treatment. The goal is to increase honesty and self-awareness each time the inventory is completed. Questions to ask can include:

- How does my addiction affect me? Include physical, emotional, financial, spiritual aspects.
- How does my addiction affect those around me? Include workplace, home, children, social situations, and role model.
- What character defects in me feed the addiction? Include defects such as insecurities, excessive pride, poor self-image, anger, and controlling behavior.

Changing character defects

Personality qualities that are referred to as "character defects" are considered to be roadblocks in the road to recovery from addiction and could diminish the quality of life of the patient. Therefore the patient should be encouraged to try to change these defects through the following steps:

- The patient should identify the qualities in his or her personality that cause problems such as

anger, impatience, or overconfidence.
- Next the patient should decide which of these qualities he has the power to change and if it would be best for him to make this change.
- Then the patient needs to make the commitment to try to change the qualities.
- If necessary, the patient needs to seek help from others.
- Finally, the patient needs to be determined to follow through on the commitment to change.

Identification and fulfillment of needs

An addict's need to get drugs has been the uppermost thing in his life. Very often other needs are not met or even recognized during addiction. He may feel that he does not have the right to have his needs met. The counselor should help the patient to identify the needs that need to be met and to introduce the various behaviors in which needs can be met. He should be encouraged to practice assertive behavior to meet needs. Frequent practice of this skill can lead to better ways to meet needs. Assertion means to stand up for one's personal rights in direct, honest, and appropriate ways. Nonassertion has to do with letting others violate one's rights. Characteristic behaviors include not being honest with others or not being assertive about expressing one's thoughts and feelings. Aggression is standing up for one's rights by dishonesty and inappropriate behavior. The goal is domination.

Managing anger
Many addicts use drugs to manage anger because the drugs numb their true feelings. Because they do not realize that they are angry, then an explosive episode of anger can occur. Many times addicts have never learned how to express anger in a healthy way. Often an addict is angry

Copyright © Mometrix Media. You have been licensed one copy of this document for personal use only. Any other reproduction or redistribution is strictly prohibited. All rights reserved.

at himself because of his drug use but blames others for the problem. The counselor should help the patient to recognize what and who causes feelings of anger. Then he needs to be able to recognize when his rights have been violated and act in an assertive way to help avoid an angry explosion. The counselor should help the patient to know and to be able to use healthy ways of expressing anger. Time out from an argument, physical activity, and assertive communication are anger management skills. The main thing is to help the patient to be able to deal with anger without relapse.

Drug-free lifestyle

Developing a drug-free lifestyle is one of the most important parts of the lifelong recovery process.

- The addict should be encouraged to be around supportive friends and family who are drug-free. If no friends or family are available, then suggestions and encouragement as to how to make new friends should take place.
- Establishing a consistent daily schedule is another help. Structure in daily activities supports abstinence.
- The next step should be the establishment of larger goals.

Even though the philosophy of sobriety is "one day at a time", the addict can think about what things he would like to have in his life. Starting a new career, going to school, saving money for a new home, or even changing careers can be goals related to recovery. The addict and the counselor can look at methods to achieve the goal. The goal should be realistic within the context of the recovery lifestyle.

Transfer of addictive behaviors

Many times recovering addicts believe that it is a good thing to replace their addictive behavior with another behavior in which they act in just as compulsive a manner. The reason this is not helpful is because compulsive behavior take away the ability to have free choice in one's activities. One no longer has control when an activity becomes compulsive. Therefore, true sobriety in the future will not take place. The counselor should help the patient to make a structured plan so that recovery is the main priority. Planning a day so that there is a balance between work and recreation is important. Identifying and meeting needs should also be a priority. Relaxation, good nutrition, and exercise need to be part of the plan.

Motivational Enhancement Therapy

Motivational Enhancement Therapy is a planned approach to substance abuse treatment. It is basically patient-centered even though the counselor does direct the treatment. It is based on the idea of getting the patient to motivate himself for change. The patient makes the personal decision to change and then constructs a plan. Each patient sets his own goals, but the counselor can direct the patient toward abstinence and other goals related to recovery. The basis of Motivational Enhancement Therapy is that the patient will be able to see the connection between his behavior and his goals. The counselor's part in the treatment process is to get the patient to make self-motivational statements about wanting to change and making a commitment to change. Intrinsic motivation is supposed to be the necessary factor in causing a change in behavior.

Copyright © Mometrix Media. You have been licensed one copy of this document for personal use only. Any other reproduction or redistribution is strictly prohibited. All rights reserved.

Post-traumatic stress disorder and substance abuse

Research is showing that post-traumatic stress disorder is a risk factor for drug abuse. 30 to 60 percent of drug abusers show the symptoms of PTSD. Children are especially at risk. Therefore early treatment is very important. There are more severe symptoms among patients who have substance abuse problems along with the PTSD than those patients who only have PTSD. Post-traumatic stress disorder is caused by exposure to an event which is not only terrifying but can cause potential harm or perhaps did cause harm. It is classified as an anxiety disorder. PTSD can result from accidents, combat, and events to which the patient was a witness. Some of the symptoms are difficulty sleeping, avoidance of people, emotional apathy, and/or flashbacks of the event itself. Often PTSD occurs at the same time as depression and alcohol and other drug abuse. The most successful treatments occur when there is early diagnosis and intervention.

Stress and substance abuse

Stress is a natural occurrence in life for all people. However, what causes stress for some people does not affect others. Individuals react to stress in different manners also. Some may get out and run a mile while others might smoke a cigarette or drink a glass of wine. Also, some individuals are quite capable of dealing with a lot of stressors in their lives while others may need treatment. Stress is a major factor in the initiation of drug and alcohol abuse. It is also known to cause a relapse in a recovering addict. Techniques to help the person in treatment to be able to cope with stress are invaluable. Not only are coping skills important, but problem-solving skills along with support groups help treatment to be successful. Recovering addicts should develop healthy ways to deal with the everyday stresses of life and even critical periods of stress.

Short and long-term treatment programs

Short-term treatment programs do not last longer than six months. Medication therapy, residential therapy, and drug-free outpatient therapy are all short term treatments. Short term residential treatment lasts from three to six months within a residential setting followed by outpatient therapy and attendance in self-help groups such as AA. Long term treatment programs include methadone maintenance, outpatient treatment for opiate addicts, and residential therapeutic community treatment. Methadone maintenance for heroin addicts will include the administering of an oral dose of a synthetic drug which mimics the effects of heroin. Out-patient drug free treatment is medication free and involves programs for the addict at clinics. Therapeutic communities are residential treatments lasting from six to twelve months.

Transference and countertransference

Transference is a situation wherein a client transfers how he feels about important people in his life to the counselor. This can cause a problem in how the client sees and responds to the counselor. He also loses his objectivity. Transference can produce both positive and negative effects. It can also grow in intensity as treatment progresses. Therefore, the counselor's plan is to make use of the transference. Countertransference is how the counselor feels about the clients. It can be harmful if it uncovers blind spots within the counselor. The feeling or attitudes of the counselor can be real, transferred, or responses to other situations. If countertransference is not identified and dealt with, it can cause the counselor to

Copyright © Mometrix Media. You have been licensed one copy of this document for personal use only. Any other reproduction or redistribution is strictly prohibited. All rights reserved.

use interventions that are not helpful to the client as well as the use of the client for gratification. It is an area which needs specific supervision.

Listening responses

Listening responses are the basis for other treatment strategies. There are three processes:
- Receiving the message from the client
- Processing the message
- Returning a message to the client.

Maintaining good eye contact and maintaining a professional look which includes sitting up straight in a relaxed and open style are both important listening skills. Clarifying what the client has said is one way to respond to his message. Restating or paraphrasing what has been said is another skill which can let the client know that he is being heard. Reflection is similar to paraphrasing, but it adds an emotional tone to the client's words. It can be used in the therapy session to help the client to feel understood. Also, it helps him to be able to express his feelings. Negative feelings can be spread out.

Action responses

Action responses can be probes or questions, confrontation, or interpretation. An important note for use of action responses is timing. Use should be determined upon the establishment of a relationship. Probes and questions should be based on the concerns of the client. Also, they should be open-ended and non-judgmental. Confrontation occurs when the counselor points out mixed messages and faulty responses from the client. The confrontation should not be in the form of an accusation but rather a challenge. Interpretation provides the client with the experience of looking at himself in a new way. It can provide an insight into different causes of behavior. Steps in interpretation are:
- Listening and identifying implicit meanings
- Forming an interpretation
- Selecting words that are similar to the client's
- Observing the client for non-verbal recognition

Non-verbal responses

Non-verbal responses are all the ways that humans react without speaking. They provide a form of valid communication which is not intentional. Some common interpretations of non-verbal responses are as follows:
- Brows are lowered over the eyes - anger
- Eyebrows are raised high - surprise
- Smile - happiness
- Tight lips - anger or frustration
- Head shaking - anger
- Nodding of head - agreement
- Arms folded over chest - avoidance or refusal to give information
- Hands perspiring - anxiety
- Shuffling or tapping of feet - impatience or anxiety
- Repeated crossing of legs - depression, anxiety, impatience
- Fear is expressed in the eyes

Discrepancies between the non-verbal responses and what the client may be saying can give the counselor insight into what is going on with the client.

Crisis counseling

Crisis counseling refers to a time in which the client is facing complete upheaval of his world coupled with extreme frustration. Being able to cope is out of the question. Extreme dysfunction is

Copyright © Mometrix Media. You have been licensed one copy of this document for personal use only. Any other reproduction or redistribution is strictly prohibited. All rights reserved.

present. These times are only temporary but can lead to long-term negative consequences. There are three categories of stressors (crises) which are external factors, internal distress, and transitional states. Examples of external factors are death of a loved one, loss of a job, surgery, natural disaster, terrorism, or any other extreme loss. Internal distress includes depression, hopelessness, thoughts of suicide, post-traumatic stress, and/or bad drug reactions. Examples of transitional states might be moving to a new location, the arrival of a new family member, illness, retirement, conflict within the family, or a family member that is gone. The goal of crisis counseling should be short-term solutions for the problem.

Suicide assessment

Suicide assessment is made up of four components:
- First are the behavioral indications. Look for giving away of special items, making plans and getting affairs organized, statements regarding feelings of worthlessness, verbal threats, and ongoing depression.
- Next are the historical patterns which include a family history of suicide, previous attempts at suicide, recent widowhood or loss of job, or a history of more than one trauma.
- Third is the present situation. Look for recent substance abuse, chronic depression, poor control of impulses, acute stress, recent loss which is significant, and/or strong feelings of hopelessness.
- In assessing the degree of lethality, several factors are important and are as follows: specific and current plans of suicide, access to or a plan to get tools for suicide, timetable, location, and commitment.

Suicide intervention

The following are some strategies to intervene or prevent a suicide:
- Take threats seriously.
- Stay calm.
- Deal with what is happening right now.
- Make local resources available.
- Tell the client you must report the threat to authorities.
- Try to get the client to make a written promise to contact the counselor before doing anything harmful.
- Let the family know what is going on so that they can help.
- Try to increase the support system of the client.
- Arrange to put this support system into action.
- Decide how serious the intent is.
- Let the client talk all he needs to.
- Don't try to make the client feel better or to think things are not so bad.
- Arrange to check on the client at a particular time.
- Talk with one's supervisor.
- Get some help (refer) if the situation cannot be handled.
- Document everything that is said and done.

Intervention preparation

The first thing to be done in the intervention preparation is the development of a list by each team member. The lists should contain non-judgmental expressions of care and concern, specific information about time, when, where, how much, and what the client was drinking, descriptions of actions and reactions, and a final concluding statement of care. Next, an action plan should be designed. This should be the step-by-step procedure of intervention. Include where the

Copyright © Mometrix Media. You have been licensed one copy of this document for personal use only. Any other reproduction or redistribution is strictly prohibited. All rights reserved.

intervention will take place, who will transport, and what time it will take place. Then plan the seating arrangement, ground rules, order in which lists will be shared. Finally, an offer of help should be made. The decision regarding where the client will go is made by the team based on the needs of the client. Arrangements should be made before the offer of help is extended. It is then the choice of the client as to whether he will accept this help.

Diverse populations

Effective counseling can be present if the counselor has a knowledge of, racial and ethnic cultures, different lifestyles, age, gender, and the needs of people with disabilities as related to how these things affect behavior and addiction. Knowledge of assessment techniques that are appropriate to the client's sex and culture is also very helpful. Finally, a knowledge of the legislation that is linked to human, civil, and client rights as well as The Americans with Disabilities Act improves counseling. The client's knowledge of English, socio-economic status, and the roles of males and females within his culture are important factors for the counselor to be aware of. Certain considerations in the treatment of women clients are important. These include focusing attention on the role of the woman as a mother and a look at the possible presence of physical and/or sexual abuse.

Adolescent clients

Some of the considerations that should be taken when an adolescent is the client are as follows:
- Peers are extremely important
- Age of risk-taking

- Period of growth when change and adjustment are characteristics
- Adolescents think everyone is interested in what they are doing

Things that could be risk factors for chemical abuse:
- Adolescents know little about the consequences of abuse.
- Low self-esteem
- Low self -confidence
- The presence of anxiety
- The presence of pessimism
- When the adolescent is impassive
- When there is a strong need for acceptance by peers and others.
- Rebellion
- School work is poor
- Adolescent has alienated himself from social values.
- If there is pro-drug use pressure from family or peers
- If the parents indicate a tolerance for drug use
- Others in the family have used drugs.

Effects of chemical dependency on development
The effects of chemical dependency on adolescent development are as follows:
- Chemical dependency causes a continuing of personal fable thinking and distorted cognition during the adolescent development of cognition.
- It also interferes with the maturation of abstract thinking.
- The development of reasoning and thinking skills is impaired.
- Problems with recall and short-term memory are seen.
- Adolescents who use drugs are more prone to use avoidance rather than language to deal with conflict.
- Academic performance is poor which affects language skills. The

Copyright © Mometrix Media. You have been licensed one copy of this document for personal use only. Any other reproduction or redistribution is strictly prohibited. All rights reserved.

lack of adequate language skills can cause the adolescent not to take part in treatment or to get any benefits.

Physical development is affected in the following ways

- Adolescents avoid their uncomfortable feelings about sexual development.
- The development of secondary sex characteristics can be interfered with by early use of marijuana. Inaccurate sexual information is obtained.
- Inadequate ways to channel sexual energy are present. They do not know how to control their sexual urges.
- Also, there is confusion about sex roles.

The role of the family in connection with adolescent development is seen when an adolescent uses drugs to declare his independence but in so doing makes sure that his parents will continue to exert control. His actions insure that nobody will believe that he is competent and further dependence on the family is insured. Disagreements over substance abuse prevent peacemaking.

Social and emotional development are affected in the following ways: The adolescent relies on drugs rather than people for a primary relationship. He is usually involved with a peer group who only think of themselves. Rules, mores and values are avoided. He tries to protect himself against fear, anxiety, and vulnerability by acting "big" and blaming others.

Adolescents are academic underachievers who have a low energy level toward school. They have an immature attitude regarding having to do things they

consider boring. Finally, they do not appreciate the need to set goals.

Primary developmental tasks
The primary developmental tasks of adolescence and some of the characteristics of each are:

- Separation and individualization - An identity that is completely separate from the parents is established. Personal boundaries are established.
- Psychosexual development - A comfortableness with body image and changes that occur psychologically develops. An ability to be intimate is established.
- Development of a sense of meaning and purpose - A spiritual base and set of values is developed. Relationships with adults are established.
- Development of social competencies - Social problem solving skills, controlling impulses, and self-confidence are mastered. Development of feelings of empathy for others and skills to maintain friendships
- Development of cognition and language – The ability to have abstract thinking is developed. Problem solving skills are developed. The ability to express oneself with abstract ideas and thoughts is developed.

Youth at risk for addiction
An adolescent must develop and master several tasks in order to be able to make the step into adulthood successfully. Experimentation with "adult behaviors" typically takes place including the experimentation with chemicals. Nine out of ten seniors in high school have experimented with alcohol. There is a high suicide rate among adolescents, and

Copyright © Mometrix Media. You have been licensed one copy of this document for personal use only. Any other reproduction or redistribution is strictly prohibited. All rights reserved.

67% of the suicides had drug use as a factor.

NAADAC's position on this problem is that:
- Money should be appropriated specifically to design programs for the prevention of chemical abuse of adolescents.
- In addition, money should be appropriated for treatment of adolescents which needs to be completely different than adult treatment.
- Finally, media advertising of alcohol should be strongly regulated.

Developmental model of adolescent recovery

There are seven phases of adolescent recovery:
- Pretreatment phase
  - Come to the realization that unpleasant things have occurred as a result of their drug use.
  - Emotional pain is a motivating factor in wanting treatment.
  - A decision to seek treatment is usually made.
- Initial stabilization
  - The routine surrounding using drugs is interrupted.
  - Abstinence occurs, which lets recovery from withdrawal take place.
- Early phase recovery--Phase 1
  - Understanding and accepting addiction 2. Triggers identified
  - Personal responsibility is assumed
- Early phase recovery—Phase 2
  - Management of triggers and cravings
  - Issues which caused use are addressed.
- Middle phase recovery--(6-12 months)
  - New behaviors are developed. 2. Committed to recovery
  - Develops balance in life
- Advanced phase--(12-18 months)
  - Coping mechanisms are learned.
  - Independence from treatment developed
  - Healthy relationships developed
- Maintenance phase
  - Spiritual development
  - Personal growth
  - Recovery is not their entire life now.

Elderly clients

Some of the considerations that should be taken when dealing with elderly clients are to understand that the effects of any drug might be more striking when given to an elderly patient. Tolerance and unwholesome effects are highly affected by age-related changes. Two types of substance abusers among the elderly have been noted--those who have abused drugs all their life and those who have recently started the abuse. The following are signs that an elder might be abusing drugs:
- Loss of memory
- Falls and fractures that are frequent
- Confusion
- Seizures that have just begun
- Abnormal liver
- Daily use of the substance.

Things to consider regarding treatment should include medical support, dietary supplements, housing and family problems and dual disorder treatment. Treatment plans should be made in the context of how people adjust to aging. After treatment, follow-up and outreach need to be provided.

Copyright © Mometrix Media. You have been licensed one copy of this document for personal use only. Any other reproduction or redistribution is strictly prohibited. All rights reserved.

Alcohol

Research has shown that between two and ten percent of persons in the U.S. who are 65 or older are addicted to alcohol. Further information indicates that one out of every five persons who is being treated for a medical or psychiatric problem is also having problems with alcohol. Doctors are known to identify physical and mental conditions caused by the abuse of alcohol as related to age only. These symptoms are usually associated with aging so that it is natural. Also signs of alcoholism are masked by prescription drugs used a lot by the elderly. Elderly alcoholics are many times ignored by health care workers, and family members are embarrassed to bring the problem out into the open. Therefore, it can go untreated until the person possibly gets arrested for DWI. NAADAC believes that education for the medical community should take place as well as increasing the availability of affordable treatment services for the elderly.

Abuse of prescription drugs

Large numbers of elderly people are using prescription drugs such as benzodiazepines, sedatives and hypnotics without the close supervision of doctors:

- The abuse of these drugs can affect the way that they are metabolized in the body, the interaction with alcohol, and interactions with other drugs.
- The ability to think and function is diminished. Therefore, the likelihood of falling and being put into an institution increases.
- Dementia and delirium that are drug related are often diagnosed as Alzheimer's.
- Older people experience an increase in the severity of the side effects of these prescribed drugs. Memory, attention, and daytime sleeping are affected.

Very little narcotic or opiate abuse is present in the elderly population. The majority of people who are prescribed narcotics or opiates do not become dependent.

Barriers to identification and treatment of problems

The following barriers prevent effective identification and treatment of substance abuse among the elderly:

- Ageism is the idea that the problems of older people are just part of getting old. Therefore the searching for a medical, social or psychological cause of a problem does not take place. This mind set is based on the idea that getting old is not something to look forward to.
- Another barrier is lack of awareness. This lack of awareness refers to the signs of alcohol abuse by the client or his family.
- The behavior of clinicians and service professionals is another barrier to treatment. They are often slow to identify the problem of substance abuse in the elderly. This is due to the fact that many of the symptoms of aging as well as substance abuse are the same.
- The existence of both medical and psychiatric conditions hampers the diagnosis.
- Lack of transportation can be a barrier to the identification and/or treatment of an elderly substance abuser.
- While getting to a hospital might not be a problem, getting to a group support meeting such as AA might be difficult. This difficulty is especially great in rural areas or where public transportation might be dangerous.
- Shrinking social support network means that there are fewer

Copyright © Mometrix Media. You have been licensed one copy of this document for personal use only. Any other reproduction or redistribution is strictly prohibited. All rights reserved.

friends available for support, transportation, or participation in the treatment.
- Lack of time to devote to treatment may be a problem.
- Many times the older patient has to help with other family members such as grandchildren while their parents work.
- Many programs do not have professionals that specialize in treatment of the elderly. Also, these programs are not set up to deal with the problems of the elderly such as loss of hearing.
- Finally, the way insurance policies are set up can be a financial barrier to the elderly.

Treatment obstacles of older women
Older women face specific barriers to treatment because:
- Less research has been done on them as group
- They make up the minority of older substance abusers.
- They hide the fact that a problem exists
- More of these women living alone which makes identification difficult.
- They have less insurance coverage and supplemental income.
- They do not drink in public places and are less likely to drive while intoxicated. Often, older women do not drive. Many drink alone at home where they are isolated from others.
- Women are prescribed psychoactive drugs more frequently than men and are more likely to become long-term users.

Treatment obstacles for racial and ethnic minority groups
The following treatment obstacles do exist for older people belonging to racial and ethnic minority groups:

- Research has discovered that there is an increase in drinking among this group, especially those of African American backgrounds.
- Medical treatment occurs in busy hospitals where alcohol and drug abuse issues are rarely addressed.
- Many times language is an obstacle because these people do not speak English. If interpreters are used, they can bias the communication which can be another obstacle to treatment.
- Often there is a lack of cultural competence present in the providers of treatment and therapy. This presents an obstacle for effective treatment for non-English speaking patients. The provider should have a working knowledge of the beliefs of his patient in order to be able to interview and interpret the way he responds.

Treatment obstacles for homebound persons
Identification and treatment of substance abuse among homebound elderly adults has the most obstacles:
- This group is homebound because of the many medical problems such as heart disease, diabetes, and lung disease. These conditions cause the older adult to limit his activities to the extent that seeking treatment for substance abuse is unlikely.
- These persons are at high risk for alcoholism because of their isolation.
- Another problem incurred is the difficulty of transportation caused by the health conditions. Getting out of the home is so difficult and tiring.
- It always requires the assistance of another person. This condition creates a feeling of dependency

- 52 -

Copyright © Mometrix Media. You have been licensed one copy of this document for personal use only. Any other reproduction or redistribution is strictly prohibited. All rights reserved.

that can lead to alcohol abuse. Being homebound causes an isolation of the individual to occur. Lack of detection of any substance abuse can then take place.

- Depression and hopelessness are conditions which can develop in these elderly, homebound adults.

NAADAC recommendations for women's issues

The recommendations of NAADAC regarding women's issues in chemical dependency are as follows:

- Supports legislation that requires all advertisement (printed and media) of alcohol to carry a warning about the dangers of alcohol use, including use during pregnancy.
- Supports equality of funding for research on alcohol abuse by women including ethnic and racial, socioeconomic, sexual preference and age groups
- Training regarding women's issues specific to substance abuse for certification including items that are related to this topic to be included on the licensing exams
- Belief that women's and men's dependency on drugs is different; therefore, the treatment of the two should be different
- Provision of services to treat women from all walks of life, provision of childcare for women in treatment, and the provision of services which include detox, residential care both short and long term, and nonresidential care
- Provision of immediate treatment for women who are pregnant
- Increasing the resources for treatment of older women

Relapse differences between men and women

Several differences have been noted between men and women as related to relapse into substance abuse:

- Women do not have relapses as frequently as men do. This may happen because women are more prone to take part in group therapy.
- It is believed that women are more willing than men to seek treatment.
- Also, there are differences in what causes cocaine-addicted men and women to relapse. This leads to the belief that possibly different relapse prevention strategies should be used when treating men and women.
- One idea as to why this might be true is the belief that women are more highly motivated to change their behavior because of the stigma of substance abuse as well as child care difficulties.
- Women who go into treatment have to be willing to overcome many more barriers than men.

Differences in reasons for relapse have been noted between men and women:

- Women have said that prior to relapse they experience negative emotions and problems with others, whereas men report positive experiences before going into relapse.
- Men felt like they were entitled to use drugs, but women returned to drug use on impulse. Greater numbers of women said that they began using drugs again almost immediately after the thought occurred.

Copyright © Mometrix Media. You have been licensed one copy of this document for personal use only. Any other reproduction or redistribution is strictly prohibited. All rights reserved.

Different strategies of treatment can be used for men and women based on these differences:

- Ways to deal more effectively with negative emotions and problems with others might be more useful for women. Getting control of situations before they get out of hand is a way of coping with this problem.
- Men, on the other hand, might need some help in the area of not letting down their guard against relapse when they are feeling good.

Relationship between women and alcohol

The relationship between women and alcohol, according to Sheila Blame, M.D., CAC, is described below:

- Depression in women can cause alcoholism. On the other hand, depression is often a result of alcoholism in men.
- The effects of alcohol are greater in women even though they drink less than men. This is true because alcohol is distributed throughout the total body of water in a human. Women weigh less; therefore, the alcohol is more concentrated.
- The effects of alcohol are less predictable in women because there is a variance in the peak levels of blood alcohol from day to day.
- A woman's normal sex response is depressed by alcohol.
- Women grow dependent on alcohol later in life than men, but dependence grows more quickly.
- Health problems due to alcoholism develop with shorter histories of abuse and lower levels of intake.

- Prescription drug abuse and alcohol abuse are more likely in women.
- Alcoholism causes women to have a higher death rate.

Peter Bell's model for counseling black clients

The model used by Peter Bell in counseling black clients is useful in the treatment of all clients who come from different value systems, life styles or backgrounds. These clients would fall into four categories:

- Acculturated - An individual who is identified as acculturated mainly identifies with the norms of the white middle class even though he might be African American. He would have no links with any part of his ethnic group.
- Bi-cultural - The bi-cultural individual would be proud of his ethnic group but would largely identify with the norms of the white middle class.
- Culturally immersed - A person who is classified as culturally immersed is most often seen as militant because he is so "pro - whatever ethnic group he is from". The individuals live, play, and work with people that are just like themselves.
- Traditional-interpersonal - These people rarely have contact with others outside their group.

NAADAC position on ethnic affairs

NAADAC is concerned with making the treatment of individuals from diverse backgrounds effective. The following issues must be considered in order to achieve a higher degree of success:

- Staff members need to be multi-cultural.

Copyright © Mometrix Media. You have been licensed one copy of this document for personal use only. Any other reproduction or redistribution is strictly prohibited. All rights reserved.

- Tools for assessment should be representative of many different cultures.
- Media which is used in treatment should represent many cultures.
- Support groups need to address the values of many cultures.
- Effective treatment should address the whole individual - cultural, emotional, psychological, physical, social, and spiritual

Education and implementation of programs which address the cultural differences and unique qualities of all people can only improve the treatment of these individuals. NAADAC sees the role of its Ethnic Affairs Committee as an advocate and provider of sources for counselors so that they can more adequately treat their multi-cultural patients.

NAADAC position on lesbian, gay, and bisexual substance abusers

NAADAC understands that lesbian, gay, and bisexual persons not only deal with problems related to their sexual orientation but also from their diverse multi-cultural backgrounds. Counselors need to recognize and understand these issues so that prevention and treatment of chemical abuse will not be complicated. NAADAC does not believe that homosexuality causes alcohol and drug abuse. It does believe that homosexual persons tend to use drugs more frequently to lessen the feelings of being stigmatized by society. NAADAC advises counselors to be aware of the bias, prejudice, and bigotry towards homosexuals which may complicate treatment and recovery. NAADAC advises against trying to change anyone's sexual orientation. NAADAC advise counselors to be very mindful to the problems of children of homosexual parents.

HIV counseling and prevention

HIV counseling for the treatment and prevention of the disease requires several approaches which are dependent on the strengths of the treatment providers and what kinds of treatment settings are available. Treatment of the addiction of HIV patients has been shown to be effective in reducing the spread of HIV. The treatment can help boost self-esteem. Tests for HIV should be a part of all addiction treatment. Counselors should encourage clients who have HIV and addiction problems to attend support groups for both diseases. Precautions should be the same in treatment programs as they are in hospital and clinic settings. Clients should be encouraged to have T cell counts periodically and to start anti-retro viral therapy. Finally, counselors should be aware of the psychiatric symptoms which can be present in HIV and addictive clients such as insomnia, dementia, personality disorders, and depression.

AIDS and drug abuse

The problems of AIDS as related to drug abuse are:
- HIV infection is spread largely by behavior which is connected to drug abuse.
- AIDS is a disease which causes individuals to be susceptible to diseases because their immune system is defective. There is no cure.
- The sharing of needles, cotton swabs, water, and cookers to use heroin and cocaine increases the chances of transmitting or acquiring the disease.
- The use of drugs also causes the risk of getting AIDs to increase because the use lowers judgment about sexual behavior. Most of the new HIV positive persons are

Copyright © Mometrix Media. You have been licensed one copy of this document for personal use only. Any other reproduction or redistribution is strictly prohibited. All rights reserved.

also injecting drug abusers. An average of 27% of the injecting drug abusers have HIV.

Education and community outreach programs which target the at risk individuals can possible reduce or eliminate the behaviors such as needle sharing of drug abusers.

Dual disorders

Dual disorders means the presence of two medical disorders that are independent but interactive. There are three ideas about treating dual disorders, which are sequential treatment, parallel treatment, and integrated treatment. Sequential treatment is characterized by treating one disorder followed by the second. Parallel treatment means treatment for both disorders at the same time. This involves two separate treatment programs. Integrated treatment means that one program treats both disorders. Some of the issues in treatment that need to be addressed are as follows:

- A personal relationship with the client
- Helping with food, housing, etc.
- Helping with finding a job
- Using commitment that may be involuntary if necessary
- Help with child care
- Working toward a broad scope of treatment
- Working toward a continuity of treatment
- Finding ways to motivate
- Finding ways to treat clients are different levels.

The phases of dual disorder treatment are short-term, sub-acute stabilization, and long-term stabilization.

Group counseling

Group counseling or group therapy is one of the most common treatment models for substance abuse, but little is known about its effectiveness. Its focus is usually on one type of problem such as addiction. Some of the good things that group therapy does are:

- Provides hope
- Shows that others have experienced the same things
- Gives advice
- Shows that one can receive good things by giving
- Provides a group format to discuss family issues
- Learning behaviors through watching others.

Two important professional issues to consider are to make sure that the clients are informed about the group process and therefore have given an informed consent and to emphasize the importance of confidentiality.

Group growth

The first stage of group growth is called Developing, which is divided into two substages called Acquaintance and Groundwork:

- The Acquaintance period is a time of people being introduced to a group of total strangers. Further, they have to share very personal moments with these strangers. This creates a very threatening atmosphere.
- Groundwork stage is a time of conflict about authority, and tensions run high.

Stage II is called Potency and is made up of two substages called Working and Closing.

- During Working, conflict is discovered to be just a cause of

Copyright © Mometrix Media. You have been licensed one copy of this document for personal use only. Any other reproduction or redistribution is strictly prohibited. All rights reserved.

problems. Therefore, it is resolved and cohesion of the members is developed. Most of the work can be done during this stage because it carries a sense of accomplishment.

- Groups normally do not get to the Closing Stage because the members feel that continuation of the group is not necessary.

Support and therapy groups

Therapy groups working with support groups are the most beneficial method of treatment.

Therapy Groups:
- Screened membership
- Limited size
- Focus is on process

Support Groups:
- Open membership
- Unlimited size
- Focus is on content

Educating the client, family, and community

The education of the client, family, and community concerning the risks of substance abuse is one of the most important jobs of the counselor. The following elements need to be included in the plan:

- Formal and informal education based on cultural background which informs and supports substance abuse prevention and recovery.
- Description of the factors which cause individuals, communities, or groups to be at risk for substance abuse
- Information to help others to become sensitive to gender, age, and cultural backgrounds in order to prevent substance abuse

- Knowledge of the symptoms, warning signs, and the course of substance abuse
- Knowledge of resources that are available for help
- Knowledge of the principles of the prevention, treatment and recovery of substance abuse
- Information about the relationship of other disorders and substance abuse
- Education of individuals about things like stress management, assertiveness training, saying no, ways to relax and communication skills

Indigent clients, maintaining clients before treatment, and outpatient programs

Increasing resources for indigent clients is an issue to be addressed. There are publicly-funded facilities that exist, and these might be helpful for indigent clients so it is important to know their locations. Develop a relationship with the staff at these facilities. Be aware that during certain times of the year there are more openings available in facilities. When help is found for an indigent client, choose the one who will profit the most. Factors for maintaining clients in the community while waiting for treatment include a utilization of the waiting period to prepare the client and family for what to expect in treatment. Require the client to start attending self-help groups, set up an abstinence contract, and outline the consequences of further drug abuse. Use outpatient programs for indigent programs. Persons who have had inpatient treatment or who do not have a severe abuse problem are ideal candidates.

Copyright © Mometrix Media. You have been licensed one copy of this document for personal use only. Any other reproduction or redistribution is strictly prohibited. All rights reserved.

Detoxification, inpatient/residential programs, and intensive outpatient treatment

Detoxification is usually identified as crisis intervention and serves as a beginning for further treatment. It is designed to be medical care that helps the patient with withdrawal as well as the other problems which are associated with addiction. Normally, detoxification takes place in a hospital setting or a facility designed for treatment of addicts. Inpatient/residential programs provide 24/7 care for patients. They receive 6-12 hours a day of specialized treatment. Inpatient treatment differs from residential treatment in that it has 24 hour medical coverage rather than just medical on-call coverage. Both programs include individual and group therapy plus family counseling. Length of stay ranges around 28 days for adults. Intensive outpatient treatment is the most common treatment modality due to the high cost of inpatient/residential programs. It is comprehensive and intensive coupled with the client being able to live at home and continue working. There are usually 3-5 sessions a week for 6-12 weeks.

Important terms

- Continuum of drug use - initiation, intoxication, abuse, dependence, withdrawal, craving, relapse, and recovery
- Psychoactive substance - a chemical which can change consciousness, mood and thoughts
- Pharmacotherapy - practice of treating diseases with medication
- Behavioral self-control training - become aware of the natural processes that affect behavior and realize how to consciously change those processes

- Psychotherapy - set of techniques that are supposed to improve mental health
- Relapse prevention - the process of knowing the signs and developing a plan to prevent the return to drug use after a period of abstinence
- Multimodality - treatment that is a combination of several methods
- Interdisciplinary approach - a training process based on using more than one approach to direct or change behavior
- Collaborate - to work together with other individuals or agencies to bring about a desired result

Copyright © Mometrix Media. You have been licensed one copy of this document for personal use only. Any other reproduction or redistribution is strictly prohibited. All rights reserved.

Professional Issues

Confidentiality laws and regulations

Important points regarding the Federal Confidentiality Act are as follows:

- A client must sign a release before any information can be shared. This release must indicate exactly what information will be shared and with whom it will be shared. The release must state that this information cannot be passed on and exactly what the time frame will be and when it will no longer be effective. A client must be aware that he can revoke this release any time he wants to.
- Information regarding a client's admittance or dismissal is completely restricted.
- A client must have his rights explained to him.
- The support staff needs to understand the regulations about confidentiality.
- A visitor to a treatment center needs to be educated regarding confidentiality regulations.
- Clients in treatment centers or group therapy need to be educated.
- Counselors need to be very cautious about discussing patients in public places or where they can be heard by others.

Exceptions to the Federal Confidentiality Act

The following are exceptions to the Federal Confidentiality Act:

- Other appropriate individuals need to be notified if the counselor thinks that the client might be dangerous to himself or be a threat to others.
- Consultation can be requested, but the person consulting must abide by the guidelines regarding confidentiality.
- A counselor can consult an attorney. This is provided by federal law and professional ethics.
- A counselor can consult a doctor or get help in an emergency.
- Suspected harm or neglect of a child must be reported to the proper authorities; however, drug and alcohol use is not abuse.

These guidelines must be explained to the client.

Drug testing

NAADAC approves the use of drug testing if the following guidelines are met:

- The use of drug testing should be a means to get help for someone rather than acting as a form of punishment.
- If a drug test shows a positive result, a professional in the substance abuse field should provide an assessment of the client.
- Labs with professional expertise in drug testing should be the only ones qualified to perform drug screens.
- Employers should have a written policy regarding drug screens in place before their implementation. This policy should be made clear to all employees.
- Programs for drug screens should include blood tests and breathalyzers for detection of alcohol.
- Random drug tests should only be used in the treatment setting. These tests should only be used as aids for recovery.

Copyright © Mometrix Media. You have been licensed one copy of this document for personal use only. Any other reproduction or redistribution is strictly prohibited. All rights reserved.

Record keeping

Accurate record keeping and documentation is an important responsibility of counselors. Federal, state, and local licensing regulations require that appropriate records are kept by healthcare professionals. The following standards provide the guidelines for this record keeping:

- Ink must be used, and the writing must be legible.
- Date of service and date of completion of the documentation must be included.
- The author must sign the documentation.
- It must be completed within established time frames.
- Documentation is the primary source used to communicate a client's course of treatment among members of the treatment team.
- Counselors are held accountable for the actions and interventions regarding clients by records that are kept.
- Records provide protection from charges of malpractice and negligence.
- The Federal Confidentiality Act requires that counselors are responsible for the maintenance of confidentiality of their clients' records.

Treatment implications regarding HIV infection and AIDS

Many individuals have an extreme fear of HIV and AIDS; therefore, counselors must learn ways to deal with this fear.

- Confidentiality of clients who have AIDS /HIV is particularly important. Documentation must be treated with discretion.
- Counselors must be aware of the need to help HIV clients in other

areas besides addiction. These areas could include locating support groups for AIDS and helping to get financial help and/or medical treatment.

- Treatment centers need to establish policies about how they will deal with patients who have AIDS/HIV. There are regulations in many states which require education and screening for clients in treatment centers who might be at risk. This is a part of the standard treatment program.
- Counselors should develop an understanding of HIV/AIDS. By understanding the disease, empathy can be developed for their clients who have it.

Quality Assurance

Quality Assurance is a means of evaluating the quality of treatment services by a facility. It also evaluates the appropriateness of these services. A system that is proactive rather than reactive will provide problem prevention, identification, and resolution along with the planning and development of programs. Plans for staff growth and development are also in place. These goals are accomplished by quality and appropriateness monitors who evaluate clinical programs, professional services, and systems. Patient care is also monitored, professional staff is organized, and programs are planned and evaluated. Other organizational functions include reviewing utilization and planning for staff growth and development. Documentation of monitor results, analysis of data, reports by agency functions, and proper action taken when problems are detected are critical needs. Important factors to consider in making Quality Assurance successful are to get the appropriate personnel involved and to make the program work through belief.

Copyright © Mometrix Media. You have been licensed one copy of this document for personal use only. Any other reproduction or redistribution is strictly prohibited. All rights reserved.

Policy and procedure

There are two components of policy and procedure for Quality Assurance. First, there should be a written plan which describes the objectives, organization, scope, method of monitoring, evaluation, and problem solving methods. The scope must include:

- Monitoring of patient care
- Performance of clinical programs and professional services
- Review of utilization
- The review of staff performance
- How programs and administration are integrated for meeting goals
- How much administrative support is present for clinical programming.

The second component of Quality Assurance is proper documentation that problems are addressed after they are identified. The problem should be addressed by the Board and responsible program. Some methods of addressing a problem can include:

- Revision of policies
- Communication of information
- Problem tracking
- Further monitoring
- Annual review
- Additional methods are the enforcing of rules and regulations and the renewal and revision of clinical privileging.

Federal Controlled Substance Act

The Federal Controlled Substance Act has one part that is especially important for counselors. Part 1304.28 deals primarily with record keeping with detoxification programs that use controlled substances:

- Close, documented monitoring is required by this act.
- The monitoring records must include name of patient, what dosage is being used, the amount

of dosage, and the methods used to identify the patients who receive the dosage.

- These records must also include inventories and dispensing logs.
- The dosages that are taken home must be monitored by recording the method of dispensing and the dosage amount.
- These records must be maintained for two years and are confidential under the Federal Confidentiality Act.

Referral, consultation, and client welfare

Professionals who are involved in the treatment of addicted individuals need to be aware of a number of factors:

- A nondiscriminatory attitude
- Knowledge of responsibility of counselor as well as client
- Competence
- Legal and moral standards
- Public statements
- Client welfare
- Confidentiality issues
- Obligations of society
- Interpersonal relationships
- Publication credits
- Remuneration.

Consultation is a very useful tool for addiction professionals. It includes a case review with a supervisor, treatment team, and/or coworkers. A consult with another professional such as a psychiatrist can help in clinical supervision as well as treatment planning. Consulting other healthcare professionals can provide valuable testing and evaluation. Finally, prevention and client welfare are very important. A knowledge of various prevention models provides part of a comprehensive prevention effort.

Copyright © Mometrix Media. You have been licensed one copy of this document for personal use only. Any other reproduction or redistribution is strictly prohibited. All rights reserved.

Prevention

Prevention is something that individuals can do to deal with the stresses and crises of life constructively. It is also a means to keep healthy people healthy. Finally it is a way to strengthen those who are at risk for developing a problem. Strategies that provide an effective foundation to prevent drug and alcohol abuse are as follows:

- Information needs to be provided which identify what drugs are and what they do.
- Social competencies need to be enhanced by helping individuals to accept and deal with their emotions, strengthen family relationships, set worthwhile goals, develop self-control and self-confidence, and to develop healthy relationships.
- Learn alternative strategies for dealing with boredom, frustrations, pain, loss of hope, and feelings of powerlessness.
- Prevention programs should focus on making alcohol and drugs less available.
- Teachers, parents, community leaders, and youth need to develop strengthening skills in order to be able to help others.

Counselor impairment

NAADAC considers counselor impairment a critical issue; therefore, they have developed a peer assistance program. Their position on this problem is as follows:

- Drug abuse is a treatable disease.
- It is a professional duty to help members of our profession who are affected by drug and alcohol abuse.
- Substance abuse professionals and their families are due

treatment, and it should be made available to them.
- Confidential help should be available to impaired professionals together with their being allowed to reenter their careers.

Treatment facilities need to consider certain things when treating impaired professionals:

- A policy needs to be in place and shared with the entire staff.
- Also, they need to have adequate insurance programs that will allow staff to be able to seek help.
- It is very important for close communication to take place between the facility and the treatment team regarding a staff member's reentry into employment.
- Finally, a continuing care plan needs to be considered very carefully.

Department of Transportation services

The Department of Transportation has set up specific guidelines for identifying, testing, and removal from dangerous types of work for their employees who have positive drug tests for mood altering substances. These guidelines are supported by NAADAC because work-related injuries and fatalities can be reduced. NAADAC also encourages the education of its professionals so that they can participate in the DOT evaluation and treatment process. This participation raises the level of care and competence of drug treatment. Professional services for substance abuse are set up by DOT. They are included in a federal law which regulates drug testing standards and procedures. They are known as SAP services. The qualifications criteria include any licensed physician, psychologist, social worker, assistance

Copyright © Mometrix Media. You have been licensed one copy of this document for personal use only. Any other reproduction or redistribution is strictly prohibited. All rights reserved.

professional, or certified addiction counselor. The SAP is not allowed to conduct the evaluation and then refer the client to an agency in which the SAP has a financial association. The goal of the SAP is to help provide a drug-free workplace.

Ethical principles

Ethical principles for the NAADAC member are:

- The NAADAC member shall not discriminate against clients or members of the profession because of their race, religion, age, gender, disability, ancestry, sexual orientation, or economic condition.
- It is his responsibility to protect the rights and dignity of the client.
- Empathy with persons who have physical disabilities should be demonstrated by providing special accommodations and services for them.
- The NAADAC member's responsibility is to maintain high standards in the services offered.
- He should keep respect for policies and functions of the agencies with whom he works but work toward their improvement if it will help the client.
- The NAADAC member shall recognize that his profession is based on certain standards of competency. --Continuing education is a component of professional competency.
- The NAADAC member must uphold any legal and accepted moral codes connected to the profession.
- Finally, the NAADAC member shall only make public statements that are facts backed up by research.

- The NAADAC member should give recognition to everyone who contributes to published material
- The NAADAC member should give recognition to the work that is the topic of the publication
- The NAADAC member should promote the protection of public health and the safety, welfare and best interest of clients.
- The NAADAC member should inform all clients regarding the code of ethics, professional loyalties, and responsibilities.
- The NAADAC member should keep the confidentiality of his client as his first obligation. No disclosure of confidential information that was obtained through teaching, practice, or investigation without the proper consent.
- Client relationships must be safeguarded so that the moral soundness of the counseling relationship is preserved.
- The client's assurance of access to reasonable treatment is also guaranteed.
- Colleagues of the NAADAC member should be treated with courtesy, respect, fairness and good faith.
- One should never offer counseling services to an individual who is being treated by another professional.
- Cooperation with professional ethics committees is required unless confidentiality would be broken.
- Remuneration or financial arrangements for professional services shall be made with the consideration of the best interest of the client first. The client needs to be informed about financial policies, and the ability of the

Copyright © Mometrix Media. You have been licensed one copy of this document for personal use only. Any other reproduction or redistribution is strictly prohibited. All rights reserved.

client to pay should be taken into consideration.

- A member should not take part in fee splitting nor should he use a relationship with clients for personal gain.
- Last, the NAADAC member should actively work for legislation to change policy regarding the opportunity for all who need treatment for substance abuse to have it.

Competence principle

The competence principle of the Ethical Standards of Alcoholism and Drug Abuse Counselors states:

- Counselors need to continue their education so that they can provide the very best professional competency.
- A counselor should be aware of his limitations and not attempt to offer services that are outside of his competency.
- A counselor should also be aware of what impairment can do to his competency and seek help to treat the impairment.
- Support of the NAADAC peer assistance programs is also required.

Experience in the field of substance abuse treatment has shown that rarely does an individual only have one type of compulsive behavior. Therefore, it becomes important that the counselor be able to treat several different types of disorders. Some of this treatment may require knowledge and training that the counselor does not have. So, it is important that the counselor obtains the necessary training to be able to provide these.

Client relationship principle

The client relationship principle of the Ethical Standards of Alcoholism and Drug Abuse Counselors states that the counselor should make sure that the client has access to effective treatment, and that the integrity of the treatment relationship is safeguarded. To further explain this:

- The counselor should provide the client with accurate and complete information about the potential professional relationship.
- The client should be informed and his agreement obtained regarding things like recording a session, the use of material obtained for training purposes, and/or observation of the session by someone else.
- The counselor should not be involved in professional relationships that might jeopardize his family, friends, or others that might be hurt by this relationship.
- The counselor should not use the relationship with the client for personal gain.
- Sexual behavior with present or former clients should never take place.
- Neither should they accept anyone as a client with whom they have had a sexual relationship.

Professional ethical decision-making

A systematic approach for professional ethical decision-making is one way to make an ethical problem easier. Address the following questions to find a solution for the problem:

- Is this problem a conflict between what I believe personally and the professional codes of conduct?

Copyright © Mometrix Media. You have been licensed one copy of this document for personal use only. Any other reproduction or redistribution is strictly prohibited. All rights reserved.

- Which principle of ethical conduct is involved?
- What is the principle based on?
- Is the conflict based on intellect, emotion, or needs?
- If a particular action or treatment is used, what are the short-term consequences?
- If a particular action or treatment is used, what are the long-term consequences?
- Would anyone be hurt by my decision?
- Would anyone be helped by my decision?
- Should interest impact the decision?
- Should feedback from someone be obtained, and if so, who?
- Can I justify this decision?

Peer assistance committee

The philosophy of the peer assistance committee of NAADAC is as follows:
- To identify substance abuse which results in impairment of professionals
- To provide assistance so that the professional can recover
- Recognize that substance abuse is a treatable disease
- Recognize that most impairments can be reversed
- Help impaired professionals to accept their impairment
- Make treatment available for professionals and their families
- Provide confidential and non-threatening reentry to workplace as soon as all parties are assured that recovery is in place

The objectives of the peer assistance committee of NAADAC are as follows:
- Establish prevention program to help mental health and reduce stress

- Provide safe and effective treatment
- Facilitate rehab
- Restore performance
- Work with Ethics Committee to address impairment
- Work toward support by other organizations
- Provide educational programs
- Motivate the reaching out for help
- Establish a support system
- Provide follow-up
- Provide technical assistance for employers

Self-referral and referral from concerned individuals

Professionals are strongly encouraged to use the self-referral process to the program. This provides early identification of substance abuse problems. The steps necessary for the self-referral process are as follows:
- The professional contacts the appropriate members of PAC who provide a RCP.
- The RCP makes arrangements to meet with the professional or the local intervenor. He assists in evaluating and making suggestions for treatment.
- The RCP continues contact with the professional
- The impaired professional and the referring person construct a written contract and treatment plan.

Referral from a concerned individual for treatment has the following characteristics. The following steps are necessary:
- The person should contact the professional first.
- Two members from PAC will evaluate the information.
- The decision for or against will be made by these members.

- 65 -

Copyright © Mometrix Media. You have been licensed one copy of this document for personal use only. Any other reproduction or redistribution is strictly prohibited. All rights reserved.

- The RCP will take part in the intervention.
- The RCP will start the assessment process.
- The RCP will continue contact with the professional.

Unsuccessful interventions and non-compliance with generic model of the Intervention and Monitoring Program Outline

The generic model for this program suggests that if a counselor denies that he has an impairment and refuses to get treatment, the following steps should be taken:

- The counselor will be notified by certified mail from the PAC in which he will be told that the assessment will proceed and that if he does not comply, it will be reported to the Ethics Committee
- The counselor will be contacted by the original intervenors.
- If the counselor agrees to get an assessment, then the assessment will proceed and treatment started if necessary. If he refuses, the Ethics Committee is notified.

If, in the beginning, the counselor contacted PAC as required, but then did not follow up with treatment, the following steps are taken:

- The counselor is asked to provide an updated treatment recommendation.
- If he complies, the incident is not reported.
- If the counselor does not comply, PAC notifies the Ethics Committee.

DOT drug testing

<u>Safety-sensitive, reasonable cause, random, return-to-duty, and follow-up</u>
Safety-sensitive refers to an employee's job description -- if he operates machinery on public roads, water, rails, or air; if he works on or maintains any of the equipment used; is an armed security guard; or is a dispatcher, traffic controller, or emergency responder.

Reasonable cause is conducted when a trained supervisor suspicions that an employee is engaging in alcohol or drug misuse. This is based on behavior and appearance.

Random refers to unannounced testing just before, during, or after engaging in safety-sensitive jobs. Return-to-duty is conducted after an employee has violated the policy regarding alcohol and drug use, tested positive, and now wants to return to work.

Follow-up is an unannounced testing on an individual who has tested positive and has returned to work. This testing is conducted for as many as 5 years.

<u>Pertinent points</u>
Pertinent points of the DOT drug-testing policy are:

- The following substances are required to be part of a drug screen: marijuana, cocaine, opiates/narcotics, amphetamines, PCP, and alcohol.
- If an employee tests positive, he will be provided the information necessary to contact a DOT counselor. The counselor who conducts the assessment and makes treatment recommendations may not refer the employee to a treatment facility that he owns or receives any financial compensation from.
- Supervisors must receive a designated amount of alcohol and drug education.
- Employees must receive education regarding signs and symptoms of impairment, sources for treatment, company policies, procedures for testing, and

- 66 -

Copyright © Mometrix Media. You have been licensed one copy of this document for personal use only. Any other reproduction or redistribution is strictly prohibited. All rights reserved.

consequences for positive tests or refusal to take tests.

- The DOT counselor (referred to as a SAP) will be the person who provides assessment, treatments, and follow-up evaluations as well as review of rehab after return to work.

Addition of alcohol to the National Drug Control Strategy

NAADAC feels that alcohol abuse should be addressed by the National Drug Control Strategy because it is a drug, even though it is legal. In addition, alcoholism is a primary chronic disease among many groups of U.S. citizens. If alcohol is labeled in connection with other drugs, it might result in an increase in support for treatment, prevention and education. Facts that legislators and public makers of policy should know are as follows:

- Millions of lives are lost because of alcohol abusers.
- Fetal Alcohol Syndrome will cause thousands of babies to have birth defects.
- Tax payers will have to pay billions of dollars due to crime, lost productivity, and social and health problems.
- Drug addicts are usually addicted to alcohol also.
- One in four families will be affected by alcohol abuse.

Copyright © Mometrix Media. You have been licensed one copy of this document for personal use only. Any other reproduction or redistribution is strictly prohibited. All rights reserved.

Practice Test

Practice Questions

1. Which of the following is the BEST description of a drug?
    a. a substance taken for a desired effect (other than food, water, or air)
    b. any substance taken for effect
    c. a substance used to produce a high
    d. a substance that can have both positive and negative effects

2. Psychoactive drugs are drugs that...
    a. alter behavior or mood.
    b. alter only mood.
    c. alter only behavior.
    d. have little or no effect on mood or behavior.

3. Which of the following is a psychoactive drug?
    a. aspirin
    b. birth control pills
    c. opium
    d. malathion

4. The magnitude of a drug's effect is...
    a. the dosage of the drug.
    b. the rate of absorption of the drug into the user's system.
    c. how intensely the user feels the drug's effects.
    d. the level of quality of the drug.

5. Which of the following is a common side effect of sniffing/snorting a drug?
    a. increased chance of infection
    b. elevated chance of overdose
    c. vein scarring
    d. damage to the nasal membrane lining

6. What does metabolism do?
    a. maintains the composition of the drug
    b. alters the composition of the drug
    c. alters the drug so it cannot be eliminated from the body
    d. maintains the peak intensity of the drug

7. How are drugs MOST often removed from the body?
    a. by vomiting
    b. through exhalation
    c. through the user's urine
    d. by pumping the stomach contents

Copyright © Mometrix Media. You have been licensed one copy of this document for personal use only. Any other reproduction or redistribution is strictly prohibited. All rights reserved.

8. What is a route of administration?
    a. the directions to a drug supplier
    b. a way to process a drug user's recovery program
    c. the way a drug acts upon the user's body
    d. the manner in which a drug enters the user's body

9. When a drug is ingested orally, which of the following BEST describes how the drug enters the bloodstream?
    a. through the lungs
    b. directly via a blood vessel
    c. through the stomach or small intestines
    d. via nasal membranes

10. Which of the following routes of administration achieves the longest-lasting results for the user?
    a. oral and nasal
    b. oral
    c. injection
    d. inhalation and nasal

11. How does a drug enter the user's bloodstream when snorted or sniffed?
    a. by entering a blood vessel directly
    b. through the membrane lining of the nasal passages
    c. through the stomach wall
    d. by passing through the small intestine

12. Why do some users prefer the route of injection for drug administration?
    a. It provides a fast and high-peak effect.
    b. It is easier to inject a drug than to take it other ways.
    c. Needles are safer to use than other routes.
    d. Injection has a lower chance of overdose.

13. How does the route of inhalation pass the drug into the user's bloodstream?
    a. by the stomach lining
    b. through a nasal membrane
    c. directly via a blood vessel
    d. through the lungs

14. A user's expectation of how a drug will make the user feel...
    a. is of little significance.
    b. can diminish a drug's intensity, but not enhance it.
    c. has a significant effect upon the user's experience of the drug.
    d. can enhance a drug's intensity, but not diminish it.

15. What do short-term effects of drug use refer to?
    a. effects while the drug is still in the user's body
    b. psychological effects prior to drug ingestion
    c. physiological effects of drug use only
    d. only psychological effects of drug use after the drug enters the user's system

Copyright © Mometrix Media. You have been licensed one copy of this document for personal use only. Any other reproduction or redistribution is strictly prohibited. All rights reserved.

16. A commonly seen physical effect of drug use is changes in…
     a. hair growth.
     b. pupil size.
     c. personal ideation.
     d. delusions.

17. What response to a drug has developed when increasing dosages of the drug are required over time to achieve the same effect as the original dosage?
     a. tolerance
     b. magnitude effect
     c. causative tolerance
     d. clinical ambivalence

18. The reliability of a drug refers to…
     a. a drug producing the expected effects when ingested by the user.
     b. the drug's ability to produce consistently the desired effects.
     c. the drug being what the user intended to purchase.
     d. the consistency of the cost per dosage.

19. Can drug use affect pregnant mothers?
     a. no, because drugs are carried only through the user's bloodstream
     b. yes, because the mother's blood circulates to the unborn baby
     c. yes, but only when drugs are ingested orally
     d. yes, but only when drugs are used with a nasal route of administration

20. Mental and growth retardation and physical deformities are common symptoms of…
     a. Fetal Alcohol Syndrome.
     b. heroin post-birth addiction.
     c. all prenatal drug use.
     d. overuse of prenatal pain killers.

21. Which of the following is the MOST commonly used sedative-hypnotic drug?
     a. anti-anxiety drugs
     b. barbiturates
     c. alcohol
     d. muscle relaxants

22. Barbiturate drugs are derived from…
     a. the cocoa bean.
     b. barbituric acid.
     c. turpentine.
     d. anaphylactic acid.

23. Why can an overdose of a barbiturate cause death?
     a. It targets the impulse-control centers of the brain.
     b. It causes a fast-acting negative effect on the kidneys.
     c. It quickly damages the liver.
     d. It can depress critical physiological functions, such as breathing.

Copyright © Mometrix Media. You have been licensed one copy of this document for personal use only. Any other reproduction or redistribution is strictly prohibited. All rights reserved.

24. Alcohol causes…
    a. decreased urination.
    b. decreased size of blood vessels near the skin.
    c. decreased blood flow to the skin.
    d. increased breathing at low levels.

25. Nicotine, amphetamines, and cocaine are types of…
    a. depressant-hypnotic drugs.
    b. barbiturates.
    c. stimulants.
    d. alcohol.

26. Narcotics are derived from…
    a. distillation.
    b. plants.
    c. barbiturates.
    d. a chemical reaction of barbiturate and stimulant.

27. Which of the following is the MOST common distinguishing characteristic of a psychedelic drug?
    a. altered perception
    b. depression
    c. increased alertness
    d. sleepiness

28. How long might the effects of a psychedelic drug last?
    a. 1-3 hours
    b. 4-6 hours
    c. 8-10 hours
    d. 12-15 hours

29. Which of the following is the psychoactive ingredient in marijuana?
    a. the opium poppy
    b. methadone
    c. tetrahydrocannabinol
    d. psilocybin

30. Marijuana is eliminated from the body mainly via…
    a. urine.
    b. feces.
    c. vomiting.
    d. sweating.

31. Which of the following is a drug often used in treatment for narcotic addition?
    a. methadone
    b. marijuana
    c. psilocybin
    d. nicotine

Copyright © Mometrix Media. You have been licensed one copy of this document for personal use only. Any other reproduction or redistribution is strictly prohibited. All rights reserved.

32. Narcotics withdrawal symptoms are sometimes described as being like….
    a. a head cold.
    b. experiencing food poisoning.
    c. feeling fatigued.
    d. having the flu.

33. A common side effect of long-term alcohol abuse that requires an increase in dosage is…
    a. dilated pupils.
    b. olfactory retardation.
    c. stomach discomfort.
    d. tolerance.

34. To which of the following has long-term cocaine use sometimes been linked?
    a. psychosis
    b. depression
    c. feelings of low self-worth
    d. schizophrenia

35. Heroin overdoses MOST often involve…
    a. a rise in blood pressure.
    b. damaged nasal membranes.
    c. depressed respiration.
    d. a heart attack.

36. Janie has bipolar disorder and is struggling to hold a job. She excessively uses alcohol to help her sleep at night and now cannot fall asleep without it. Her issue with alcohol could be said to be…
    a. secondary.
    b. primary.
    c. adjunctive.
    d. fundamental.

37. Bob's addiction to heroin has caused him to behave in ways that have distanced him from friendships, and he has entered treatment because of relationship issues. His heroin addiction could be called…
    a. secondary.
    b. primary.
    c. adjunctive.
    d. fundamental.

38. Self-medication MOST closely refers to…
    a. self-administering drugs with therapeutic intent.
    b. heeding a professional's direction in regards to medication.
    c. self-administering drugs with direction from a professional.
    d. self-medicating with illegal drugs.

Copyright © Mometrix Media. You have been licensed one copy of this document for personal use only.
Any other reproduction or redistribution is strictly prohibited. All rights reserved.

39. Which of the following is NOT a common problem of those with a substance abuse issue that would likely be addressed in treatment?
    a. relationship issues
    b. legal problems
    c. optical difficulties
    d. coping skills

40. Which of the following is a significant difference between casefinding and ongoing services?
    a. Ongoing treatment is rarely used for alcoholism.
    b. Casefinding involves only alcoholism.
    c. Ongoing services do not always include treatment, and casefinding does.
    d. Casefinding does not always include treatment, and ongoing services do.

41. Which of the following is the primary goal of the helping relationship between patient and counselor?
    a. elimination of the substance the patient is abusing
    b. education of the patient
    c. the emotional support of the patient
    d. changing the patient's behavior

42. Which of the following is NOT a common personality characteristic of counselors?
    a. empathy
    b. superior intellect
    c. respect
    d. concreteness

43. In relation to counseling, what is empathy?
    a. the ability to feel what another person is feeling
    b. being able to understand what another person is experiencing
    c. the ability to reflect one's own choices onto the patient's
    d. helping the patient to change unproductive feelings

44. Warmth…
    a. tends to cause the client to be suspicious.
    b. is an essential component in counseling.
    c. can be detrimental in counseling sessions.
    d. is nice, but not necessary in counseling.

45. Which of the following is NOT related to concreteness in counseling?
    a. theorizing about the patient's relationships
    b. focusing on the facts
    c. avoiding tangents
    d. keeping communications specific

Copyright © Mometrix Media. You have been licensed one copy of this document for personal use only. Any other reproduction or redistribution is strictly prohibited. All rights reserved.

46. Avoidance behaviors in a patient are common. Which of the following is NOT an avoidance behavior?
    a. gossiping about a loved one
    b. perseverating on a specific situation
    c. rationalizing
    d. generalizing

47. In counseling, to what does immediacy refer?
    a. getting the patient into counseling as soon as possible
    b. discussing the most critical issues first
    c. getting to the sessions on time
    d. dealing with feelings in the here and now

48. Which of the following BEST describes what a counselor does in a facilitative relationship?
    a. solves the patient's problems
    b. teaches the patient coping skills
    c. keeps the patient talking
    d. soothes the patient's hurt feelings

49. When a counselor adopts a relaxed posture, good eye-contact, and a pleasant tone of voice, the counselor is...
    a. attending.
    b. empathizing.
    c. focusing.
    d. trying to counsel.

50. How does one NOT convey an open invitation to talk in a counseling session?
    a. by listening to the patient
    b. taking steps to eliminate interruptions
    c. offer lengthy responses to what the patient says
    d. avoid judgmental comments

51. Paraphrasing involves...
    a. repetition.
    b. paraprofessional phrasing techniques.
    c. using clinical phrases during the counseling session.
    d. only listening skills.

52. In counseling, reflection usually involves...
    a. responding to the facts of the situation discussed.
    b. responding to feelings.
    c. a mirror.
    d. visual aids.

Copyright © Mometrix Media. You have been licensed one copy of this document for personal use only. Any other reproduction or redistribution is strictly prohibited. All rights reserved.

53. Why must every patient be treated differently?
    a. Patients with substance abuse are usually demanding.
    b. Every patient will have an underlying psychiatric diagnosis.
    c. Addictions cause changes to the patient's personality.
    d. Each patient is different.

54. If the counselor speaks English as a primary language, and the patient speaks English as a second language...
    a. counseling will run smoothly.
    b. it might still be best to consider using another language in counseling.
    c. it can be assumed that there will be no problems communicating.
    d. it is always best to counsel only in English.

55. Is a counselor a role model?
    a. yes
    b. no
    c. no, but a few unstable patients will see it that way
    d. maybe

56. You ask your patient about a particular painful experience when the patient struck his or her domestic partner. The patient speaks of the experience in a fact-based, rational tone. What is the patient likely doing?
    a. justifying
    b. cutting short
    c. resistance
    d. changing the focus

57. Which of the following is a critical component of individual counseling?
    a. maintaining an authoritative counselor/patient relationship
    b. that the counseling session addresses only one main focal point
    c. that only two people are present during the counseling session
    d. that counseling is done by one therapist

58. The issues of time, purpose, and confidentiality are parts of what?
    a. maintaining order in therapy
    b. addressing addiction-related psychosis
    c. dealing with addiction issues
    d. structuring the counseling relationship

59. Defining patient goals takes place during which point in counseling?
    a. when counselor and patient have become comfortable with each other
    b. during the treatment process
    c. within the assessment stage
    d. at the close of each counseling session

60. The intervention stage of treatment primarily focuses on...
    a. termination
    b. problem-solving
    c. assessment
    d. easing out of the counseling relationship

Copyright © Mometrix Media. You have been licensed one copy of this document for personal use only. Any other reproduction or redistribution is strictly prohibited. All rights reserved.

61. In group therapy, members must...
    a. all have different problems.
    b. be willing to share openly personal problems.
    c. remain quiet and orderly.
    d. all have the same problems.

62. Group dynamics are...
    a. always easy to manage.
    b. usually not a factor in successful treatment.
    c. always an issue in group therapy.
    d. a difficult issue in individual therapy.

63. In group therapy, which of the following is the BEST choice for characteristics of counselors and patients?
    a. punctuality and responsibility
    b. genuineness and a sense of humor
    c. respect and familiarity
    d. empathy and concreteness

64. In group treatment, direct communication refers to...
    a. trading roles with another person in the group.
    b. explaining why one feels the way one does about the other person.
    c. sharing one's feelings about the other person, and using the pronoun you when speaking.
    d. stating the reasons behind the question being asked.

65. What is role reversal?
    a. trading roles with another person in the group
    b. explaining why one feels the way one does
    c. sharing one's feelings about the other person
    d. stating the reasons behind the question being asked

66. A post-session technique in group therapy does what?
    a. reinforces insights
    b. helps patients ease back into their daily routines
    c. maintains order
    d. keeps patient accounting in order

67. Which of the following stages of a family dealing with substance abuse includes denial, disorganization, and solution finding?
    a. re-organization
    b. adjustment
    c. abandonment
    d. denial

68. In which stage do family members take on the responsibilities of the substance abuser?
    a. denial
    b. solution finding
    c. re-organization
    d. abandonment

Copyright © Mometrix Media. You have been licensed one copy of this document for personal use only. Any other reproduction or redistribution is strictly prohibited. All rights reserved.

69. Once a family leaves the substance abuser to build a new life…
   a. there is no hope for the abuser's reentry into the family structure.
   b. there is a chance the substance abuser will seek help.
   c. the substance abuser will always further isolate himself/herself.
   d. the family will invariably regret the decision.

70. The family effect upon treatment…
   a. is always positive.
   b. is always negative.
   c. can be both positive and negative.
   d. should be minimized as a part of the treatment plan.

71. Your patient has been in treatment for two weeks when the patient refuses further treatment. What should you do?
   a. contact family members to encourage a return to treatment
   b. continue to contact the patient in an attempt to return the patient to therapy
   c. contact the legal authorities
   d. note the patient's refusal and respect the patient's decision

72. The treatment plan should be…
   a. kept secret from everyone except the therapist and facility.
   b. developed together with both therapist and patient.
   c. developed only by the therapist.
   d. denied to the patient, even upon request after treatment has been completed.

73. What does a release of information form do?
   a. allows the therapist to transfer confidential information to the party specified by the patient
   b. gives the therapist the right to transfer patient information to whomever the therapist feels should have it
   c. releases patient information only within the treating facility
   d. keeps information about the patient private

74. Confidentiality rules do NOT include…
   a. the number of times a patient has attended therapy sessions.
   b. the patient's diagnosis.
   c. the patient's treatment plan.
   d. none of the above—confidentiality applies to all patient information.

75. When can confidentiality be breached?
   a. when the family demands it
   b. if the patient's employer requests information in writing
   c. if the patient threatens the welfare of another person
   d. when a spouse asks for it

76. The experience of substance abuse…
   a. is unique to each individual.
   b. is pretty much the same from person to person.
   c. can always be treated with standard treatment plans.
   d. is the same from female to female, but differs in males.

Copyright © Mometrix Media. You have been licensed one copy of this document for personal use only. Any other reproduction or redistribution is strictly prohibited. All rights reserved.

77. Your patient tells you that he or she sometimes loses control and abuses the patient's 5-year-old daughter. What should you do?
    a. report the abuse to the appropriate authorities
    b. maintain confidentiality and work with your patient on control issues
    c. contact a family member and urge that person to report the abuse
    d. tell your patient that if the abuse doesn't stop, you will report the patient to the authorities

78. You and your patient are attracted to each other. When can you ethically enter into a romantic relationship?
    a. only after treatment has progressed to a certain point
    b. once treatment is completed
    c. at any time
    d. never

79. Your patient is doing well in therapy and offers you a free weekend on the patient's yacht. What should you do?
    a. accept, but only if the patient accompanies you
    b. accept, but go only after treatment is completed
    c. politely decline the offer
    d. accept the gift in the spirit in which it is given and have a good time

80. Your patient does not seem to be meeting treatment goals after a substantial period of time in therapy. What should you do?
    a. terminate therapy
    b. terminate therapy and refer the patient to another therapist
    c. continue therapy
    d. document that the patient is resistant and continue with the treatment plan

81. Your patient is of a spiritual faith that is counter to your own. You should...
    a. avoid spiritual discussions.
    b. discuss the spiritual differences and continue with treatment.
    c. terminate treatment.
    d. continue with treatment, being respectful of the patient's beliefs.

82. While your patient is seeing you for a substance abuse problem, you begin to see indications of bipolar disorder. What should you do?
    a. refer to, or consult with, a clinician trained in bipolar disorder
    b. treat for the bipolar disorder as well as the substance abuse
    c. discontinue treatment
    d. continue to treat for the substance abuse problem only

83. A young person meeting with you for the first time asks if treatment will be effective for him or her. What should you say?
    a. tell the person that treatment is not always effective
    b. assure the person that treatment will work
    c. reassure the person that treatment will work if the person commits to it
    d. explain that treatment works to varying degrees for each individual patient

Copyright © Mometrix Media. You have been licensed one copy of this document for personal use only. Any other reproduction or redistribution is strictly prohibited. All rights reserved.

84. You find that recording therapy sessions works well for you. In relation to this practice, what should you do?
    a. explain the purpose of the recording, and obtain the patient's permission
    b. do not inform the patient of the recording, as this can inhibit the patient's participation in therapy
    c. tell the patient about the recordings, but only after treatment is completed
    d. tell the patient that you will be recording therapy sessions

85. Your patient tells you about a particular situation the patient is having trouble with. You know what is best for your patient to do, so you...
    a. do nothing.
    b. tell the patient what to do.
    c. facilitate discussion about the patient's options, guiding the patient to review his or her thoughts and feelings about the situation.
    d. steer the conversation in the direction of what you want the patient to do.

86. If there is a conflict between yourself and a colleague over treatment of a patient, you should...
    a. ignore it.
    b. try to resolve it amicably with the other therapist.
    c. do primarily whatever is in the best interest of the patient.
    d. report the conflict to a superior.

87. Your best friend has a drinking problem and approaches you for help overcoming his or her dependency. What should you do?
    a. draw up a treatment plan with your friend and begin therapy
    b. refer your friend to a therapist you feel would be a good fit
    c. tell your friend you can't help because of your personal relationship
    d. do nothing

88. You learn that your patient has been convicted of sexual assault in the past. As an assault survivor yourself, this is the one area in which you have difficulty being objective. What should you do?
    a. inform the patient of your situation, but continue with therapy
    b. terminate therapy
    c. continue with therapy, doing the best you can in the situation
    d. refer your patient to another therapist

89. Which of the following is the primary focus of a code of ethics?
    a. keeping the therapist out of legal trouble
    b. defining basic concepts for working with other professionals
    c. helping guide the professional in the right thing to do
    d. providing guidelines for dealing with legal issues

90. Your patient in a residential treatment program becomes agitated and is wildly striking out at everyone in the patient's path. May you physically restrain the patient?
    a. yes
    b. no
    c. only if you have written instructions from the physician
    d. only if the patient consents

Copyright © Mometrix Media. You have been licensed one copy of this document for personal use only. Any other reproduction or redistribution is strictly prohibited. All rights reserved.

91. At the beginning of therapy, which of the following does the patient NOT have the right to know?
    a. behavioral expectations of the patient
    b. the thoughts and feelings of the therapist in relation to the patient
    c. purpose of the treatment plan
    d. fees associated with therapy

92. If your patient is mentally impaired or otherwise considered incompetent, can you give treatment information to family members?
    a. yes, if they are blood relatives
    b. no, not without a release of information from the patient
    c. yes, if the family member is the patient's legal guardian
    d. no

93. John Smith was a patient of your residential program six years ago. You run into his brother at the grocery store, and he asks you if John has been in treatment. What should you do?
    a. tell him nothing
    b. say you don't know
    c. say that John is no longer in treatment, but give no details
    d. tell him that John was in treatment years ago

94. Jane Doe was a patient of yours three years ago and has since died. You run into the man you know was her husband at the local park, and he asks about his wife's treatment plan. What should you do?
    a. don't give him any information
    b. deny remembering who he is, or knowing his wife
    c. discuss her case with him
    d. tell him he'll need to provide a release of information for you to discuss his wife's case with him

95. Substance abuse counselors should work only with…
    a. ages 15 to 55.
    b. any ages.
    c. ages 10 up.
    d. ages 13 and up.

96. As regards ongoing education of counselors, substance abuse counselors…
    a. should take one educational class every five years.
    b. can choose whether or not to continue their education.
    c. do not require ongoing education.
    d. need ongoing education just like other health professionals.

97. To be a truly proficient substance abuse counselor, you must…
    a. have successfully completed your educational training.
    b. have had close relationships with substance abusers at some point in your life.
    c. have been a past substance abuser yourself.
    d. have natural ability as a therapist.

Copyright © Mometrix Media. You have been licensed one copy of this document for personal use only. Any other reproduction or redistribution is strictly prohibited. All rights reserved.

98. Substance abuse counselors tend to…
    a. work only with those in the mental health professions.
    b. work only with other substance abuse counselors.
    c. work closely with other health disciplines.
    d. work completely independently.

99. You become ill and are unable to continue treating your patients. What should you do?
    a. escalate treatment and terminate early
    b. terminate treatment
    c. make arrangements depending upon the patients' needs rather than just your own
    d. refer your patient to another therapist

100. You are asked to fill in with a patient while another counselor is away. Should you accept this request?
    a. no, never
    b. yes, always
    c. yes, depending on the circumstances
    d. only if paid at a higher rate than usual

Copyright © Mometrix Media. You have been licensed one copy of this document for personal use only. Any other reproduction or redistribution is strictly prohibited. All rights reserved.

Answer Explanations

1. A: A substance taken for a desired effect (other than food, water, or air). There are many types of drugs. Some drugs are taken for reasons that are beneficial to the user. Some are addictive, and others are not. Drugs that alter behavior and/or mood are referred to as psychoactive drugs. Whatever the type of drug, the term drug does not alone imply a substance that is illegal or harmful.

2. A: Drugs that alter behavior or mood. Many drugs have an effect upon the physiology of the user (such as birth control pills), but do not alter behavior or mood—those types of drugs would not be termed psychoactive.

3. C: Opium. Opium is a psychoactive drug because it has an effect upon the behavior and mood of the user. Aspirin and birth control pills have only a physiological impact upon the individual, and malathion is an insecticide.

4. C: How intensely the user feels the drug's effects. The intensity of the drug, or how much the user feels its effects, depends upon several factors. Generally, however, the greater the dosage, the greater the intensity of the response. The peak effect is the highest intensity level at a given dosage of the drug.

5. D: Damage to the nasal membrane lining. Snorting or sniffing a drug refers to ingesting the drug through the nose. This route of administration tends to lead to irritation of the nasal membrane, and long-term damage as well. The other three possible answers (infection, overdose, and scarring) are more common with administration of a drug through injection.

6. B: Alters the composition of the drug. Metabolism is a process by which an ingested drug is changed into a form that can be removed from the user's body. The faster the drug moves through the user's system, the sooner the effects of the drug are diminished.

7. C: Through the user's urine. Drugs most often leave the body after metabolization through the user's urine. Depending upon the level of efficiency, the liver and kidneys work together to break the drug down and excrete it out of the body through the user's urine.

8. D: The manner in which a drug enters the user's body. A route of administration is the means by which a drug is taken into the user's body. This ingestion can be accomplished in a number of ways. The most common ways to bring a drug into the bloodstream are oral, injection, and inhalation and nasal.

9. C: Through the stomach or small intestines. When a drug is taken orally, it is dissolved within the stomach and then passes through the stomach lining or small intestine to enter the bloodstream.

10. B: Oral. Many users prefer the oral route of administration because the effects of the drug tend to be experienced for a lengthier period of time. The effects of the drug might be

Copyright © Mometrix Media. You have been licensed one copy of this document for personal use only. Any other reproduction or redistribution is strictly prohibited. All rights reserved.

less intense with this route, but the duration of the effects (and ease of administration) overrides that concern for many users.

11. B: Through the membrane lining of the nasal passages. When a drug is snorted or sniffed, it collects directly upon the inner lining of the nose. These nasal passages have sensitive membranes that then absorb the drug and pass it into the user's system.

12. A: It provides a fast and high-peak effect. Some users prefer injection for two main reasons. Injection not only provides a fast means of getting the drug into the user's system, but it also allows for a higher peak intensity.

13. D: Through the lungs. When the user inhales a drug, it enters the bloodstream through the user's lungs. There can be a rapid peak effect with this method of administration, but it is far more difficult to use unnoticed.

14. C: Has a significant effect upon the user's experience of the drug. Studies have shown that one's expectation of what a drug will do has a significant effect upon how that drug is experienced by the user. For example, if the user expects the drug to have a relaxing effect, the user is likely to feel relaxed after ingesting the drug.

15. A: Effects while the drug is still in the user's body. The short-term effects of drug use can be either physiological or psychological, and vary significantly from individual to individual.

16. B: Pupil size. There are several physical effects of drug use commonly seen in users. A few of the most common, and most obvious to the alert observer, are changes in pupil size, respiration, and heart rate. Delusions and personal ideation changes are psychological in nature, and hair growth is not a common effect.

17. A: Tolerance. When a user takes a drug over a long period of time, a tolerance can develop to the drug. This tolerance makes it necessary for the dosage of the drug to be increased in order to achieve the same effects as the previous dosage.

18. C: It being what the user intended to purchase. There are many look-alike drugs and disreputable dealers in the drug trade. Therefore, it can be difficult to be assured of the quality of drugs purchased on the street. The reliability of a drug refers to the drug meeting the expectations of the buyer.

19. B: Yes, the mother's blood circulates to the unborn baby. Drug use by pregnant women can affect the unborn baby, as the blood can be carried through the mother's bloodstream to the baby. The unborn baby can also become addicted to a substance, and once born (and the drug connection removed) suffer withdrawal symptoms.

20. A: Fetal Alcohol Syndrome. Women who habitually use alcohol while pregnant can cause permanent damage to their children, including mental, growth, and physical issues.

21. C: Alcohol. Alcohol, in all its forms, slows down the body's processes and is therefore known as a depressant. It is commonly used in one of three forms: beer, wine, or distilled spirits. One of the reasons for its widespread use is that it is legally obtainable.

Copyright © Mometrix Media. You have been licensed one copy of this document for personal use only. Any other reproduction or redistribution is strictly prohibited. All rights reserved.

22. B: Barbituric acid. Barbiturate drugs are derived from barbituric acid, and there are thousands of different types. They are a type of sedative-hypnotic drug and used more often by females than by males—possibly because women are more likely to seek medical attention than men are.

23. D: It can depress critical physiological functions, such as breathing. Barbiturates pass into the brain through the bloodstream and can depress physiological functions such as breathing. If too much of a barbiturate is taken, the depressive effect can be enough to stop breathing and other functions entirely.

24. D: Increased breathing at low levels. Alcohol can cause increased breathing at low levels of ingestion, and depressed breathing at higher levels. Blood flow to the skin and blood vessels near the skin is increased, as is urination due to its effect upon the kidneys and the increased fluid levels.

25. C: Stimulants. Nicotine, amphetamines, and cocaine are all types of stimulants. Stimulants generally increase mental and/or physical function and come in a variety of forms. They tend to be absorbed quickly into the bloodstream.

26. B: Plants. Narcotics are derived from opium poppies. The poppy is a common ornamental plant that is also grown on a wide agricultural scale. It has many uses other than that of a narcotic.

27. A: Altered perception. The most common distinguishing characteristic of a psychedelic drug is that users experience an alteration of their perception of reality. Psychedelic drugs are sometimes called hallucinogens because what users experience is similar to hallucinations.

28. C: 8-10 hours. The duration of the effects of psychedelic drug use vary by type of drug, route of administration, and individual differences, but a reasonable average length of effect might be 8-10 hours.

29. C: Tetrahydrocannabinol. Tetrahydrocannabinol (or THC) is the psychoactive ingredient in marijuana. THC is a chemical found in the cannabis plant; the chemical binds with receptors in the user's brain to produce several drug-induced effects.

30. B: Feces. Marijuana is absorbed through the bloodstream and produces a short peak effect (longer if taken orally rather than smoked). It is metabolized and eliminated mostly through the user's feces, but also through the urine.

31. A: Methadone. Methadone is often used in the treatment of those with narcotic addictions. It is a synthetic narcotic, the effects of which allow the user to feel and act in a more natural manner.

32. D: Having the flu. The severity of withdrawal from a narcotic addiction depends upon how much of the drug has been used and for how long, as well as how often it has been administered. However, many people describe the withdrawal symptoms from narcotics as being similar to having the flu.

Copyright © Mometrix Media. You have been licensed one copy of this document for personal use only. Any other reproduction or redistribution is strictly prohibited. All rights reserved.

33. D: Tolerance. When alcohol is used over a long period of time, the user can develop a tolerance of the drug. This tolerance requires that the user increase the dosage in order to feel the same effects.

34. A: Psychosis. Irritability is commonly seen with cocaine use that is heavy and long-term. This tendency has even been seen to proceed to psychosis.

35. C: Depressed respiration. With a heroin overdose the user's body slows down; respiration is depressed, which eventually can lead to death.

36. A: Secondary. A secondary problem is one that exists in addition to what is causing the patient's difficulties.

37. B: Primary. A primary problem is one that, if addressed, will return the patient to normal functioning. It is the main focus of the patient's difficulties.

38. A: Self-administering drugs with therapeutic intent. Self-medication refers to an individual deciding for himself or herself what medication is needed for a problem and taking the medication without direction. Although done with therapeutic intent, the therapeutic need for the medication is not confirmed by a health professional.

39. C: Optical difficulties. Although patients with substance abuse difficulties might also have vision problems, it is not a common problem addressed in treatment.

40. D: Casefinding doesn't always include treatment, and ongoing services do. Casefinding refers to finding individuals who require treatment and encouraging them to enter into a treatment process. The individual might or might not actually enter into treatment. Ongoing services refers to those who are in treatment.

41. D: Changing the patient's behavior. The primary goal of the helping relationship is to help the patient to change the behavior that is causing the difficulties in the patient's life.

42. B: Superior intellect. Common personality characteristics of counselors are such things as empathy, respect for the patient, concreteness, warmth, genuineness, and acceptance. However, a superior intellect is not necessary for an individual to be a good counselor.

43. B: Being able to understand what another person is experiencing. In counseling, one should not be feeling what the patient is feeling, but rather have the ability to understand those feelings and communicate that understanding in a clear manner to the patient.

44. B: Is an essential component in counseling. Things like warmth, respect, and acceptance are essential in a counselor's work because every patient has the right to be treated with respect and be given the opportunity to make his or her own decisions. Warmth also helps the patient to feel more comfortable with the counselor and therefore more productive in reaching the patient's goals.

45. A: Theorizing about the patient's relationships. Concreteness in a counseling session is important because it keeps the conversation on-track and avoids wasting time on tangents and insignificant material. Staying concrete makes for a more efficient and effective counseling session.

Copyright © Mometrix Media. You have been licensed one copy of this document for personal use only. Any other reproduction or redistribution is strictly prohibited. All rights reserved.

46. B: Perseverating on a specific situation. Although perseverance is not always a productive thing, in this case it is the best choice because it describes the attention to a specific topic. When a patient is avoiding a significant topic, the patient will rationalize, generalize, or in some other way avoid the relevant issue.

47. D: Dealing with feelings in the here and now. Immediacy deals with the counselor and patient working through feelings in the counseling relationship.

48. C: Keeps the patient talking. The most basic component of a facilitative relationship is to keep the patient talking. Learning how to do this is an initial step in having positive communication and a productive therapeutic experience.

49. A: Attending. A basic counseling skill is attending. The counselor adopts a relaxed body posture, maintains eye contact with the patient, and speaks in an even, pleasant tone as a manner by which to communicate attentiveness to the patient. This helps facilitate a positive counseling relationship.

50. C: Offer lengthy responses to what the patient says. One of the best ways to facilitate conversation during a counseling session is for the counselor to keep his or her comments to a minimum and encourage opportunities for the patient to talk as much as possible.

51. A: Repetition. Paraphrasing is a useful counseling skill that involves repeating back to the patient what was said, only in a more concise manner and in the counselor's own words.

52. B: Responding to feelings. In the counseling situation, reflection of feelings is a useful tool. By carefully listening to what a patient says, and determining which feelings are likely to be present, the counselor can verbally reflect back to the patient what the patient is feeling, thus bringing those feelings out in the open for attention.

53. D: Each patient is different. Every patient must be treated differently because every patient is different. Even if two patients have a very similar set of circumstances and addiction, each will still show differences in how they react to their situation, the therapeutic situation, the conflicts in their lives, etc. Counseling techniques must be adjusted to meet the needs of each individual patient best.

54. B: It might still be best to consider using another language in counseling. Even when a patient's primary language is English, there might still be another language in which the patient is better able to express himself. Care must be given to assess not only the language used by the patient, but also use of slang, etc. that is important for the patient's ability to understand and communicate effectively.

55. A: Yes. Whether or not counselors like to see it that way, they are role models because they are commonly viewed as experts who know what is best to do in any given situation. For this reason, counselors should take steps to represent themselves well in their lives.

56. C: Resistance. Patients will often resist the counseling process, and do so in several ways. In this case, the patient is avoiding his or her feelings by rationalizing or analyzing the experience the patient is describing.

Copyright © Mometrix Media. You have been licensed one copy of this document for personal use only. Any other reproduction or redistribution is strictly prohibited. All rights reserved.

57. C: Only two people are present. Individual counseling involves two people, the counselor and the patient. Unlike family or group counseling, the sessions involve only two people and are conducted in a private setting.

58. D: Structuring the counseling relationship. Time, purpose, expectations and behavior, confidentiality, and fees are all parts of establishing the counseling relationship. This is important in order that both patient and counselor begin therapy with a common understanding.

59. C: Within the assessment stage. Defining patient goals should take place during the initial stage of counseling, when a treatment plan is determined and set in place.

60. B: Problem-solving. During the intervention period of treatment, patient and counselor are focused on solving the patient's problems as set forth in the assessment stage of counseling. It is during this time when understanding and change are sought.

61. B: Be willing to share openly personal problems. In group therapy, the sharing of personal thoughts and feelings is critical if the group members are to be able to help each other through the counseling process.

62. C: Always an issue in group therapy. Group dynamics are factors that affect the counseling process. These factors can be emotional, psychological, personality factors, or any other issues that affect the interaction of the group members.

63. D: Empathy and concreteness. The four best choices of personality characteristics (of both patients and counselors) are empathy, concreteness, genuineness, and respect. Although there are many other useful characteristics as well, these four are key.

64. C: Sharing one's feelings about the other person, and using the pronoun 'you' when speaking. Direct communication involves speaking directly to the other person, rather than about him or her. The answer in d refers to the principle of question analysis, b is about advice analysis, and answer a refers to role reversal.

65. A: Trading roles with another person in the group. This technique can help group members understand why a particular member thinks, acts, and feels the way he or she does. It involves two members pretending to be the other, and sharing their viewpoints within that role.

66. A: Reinforces insights. The post-session technique in group therapy allows for patients to stay after the group therapy session and discuss the insights gained that day in treatment. It is also a good way to minimize tensions or other miscellaneous issues that came up as a result of therapy.

67. B: Adjustment. A family dealing with substance abuse often goes through stages of adjustment. These stages include denial, solution finding, disorganization, re-organization, and abandonment.

68. C: Re-organization. In a need for stability, the family of a substance abuser might begin to re-organize the family structure. Various members might take on the roles and responsibilities of the substance abuser to return order to the family.

Copyright © Mometrix Media. You have been licensed one copy of this document for personal use only. Any other reproduction or redistribution is strictly prohibited. All rights reserved.

69. B: There is a chance the substance abuser will seek help. When the family finally decides they can no longer sustain the presence of the substance abuser, the family will seek to build a new life without that family member. At this point there is still a chance of the abuser seeking help when faced with the loss of family.

70. C: Can be both positive and negative. Family can provide a great deal of support to the substance abuser. However, the negative effects of the abuser's behavior on the family can also present some unique stresses to be dealt with in treatment. A sound treatment plan takes both the positive and negative into account.

71. D: Note the patient's refusal and respect the patient's decision. A patient has a right to refuse treatment unless there are extenuating circumstances (such as a legal court order). In such a case, the therapist should make the appropriate documentation and respect the patient's decision.

72. B: Developed together with both therapist and patient. Treatment plans should be developed by the therapist and patient together, and the patient has a right to request a copy of the patient's personal records.

73. A: Allows the therapist to transfer confidential information to the party specified by the patient. A release of information form is a written form that the patient signs and in which the patient specifies to whom the confidential information can be released.

74. D: None of the above—confidentiality applies to all patient information. Any and all information about the patient is held to be confidential and must be protected.

75. C: If the patient threatens the welfare of another person. There are several times when confidentiality can be breached without the consent of the patient. One such situation is when another's life is at risk.

76. A: Is unique to each individual. The experience of substance abuse, although clinically similar in some respects among patients, is always unique to the individual. Every person has a unique situation, reaction to addiction, coping skills, etc.; therefore, treatment must be approached in a manner that is specific to each individual patient.

77. A: Report the abuse to the appropriate authorities. Although confidentiality is certainly to be protected, there are a few specific situations where it must be broken. The abuse of a minor is one such situation where it is permissible to break confidentiality.

78. D: Never. It is not considered ethical to enter into a romantic relationship with current or former patients. Patients are vulnerable and that should be kept in mind when considering any personal involvement outside the professional relationship.

79. C: Politely decline the offer. Accepting gifts, especially extravagant ones, from a patient is considered unethical. Patients are vulnerable and easily exploited, but such a situation also can detract from the respectful relationship of equals that should exist in the professional relationship.

80. B: Terminate therapy and refer the patient to another therapist. The therapist has an ethical responsibility to terminate therapy when treatment is not effective. When

- 88 -

Copyright © Mometrix Media. You have been licensed one copy of this document for personal use only. Any other reproduction or redistribution is strictly prohibited. All rights reserved.

terminating, the therapist should also take steps to refer the patient to another clinician who might better be able to work with the patient.

81. D: Continue with treatment, being respectful of the patient's beliefs. A patient's belief system should be respected, and a competent professional should be able to work with a patient regardless of that belief system. If this is not possible, then the patient should be referred to another practitioner.

82. A: Refer to, or consult with, a clinician trained in bipolar disorder. A therapist should never treat a patient for something the therapist is not trained in. In this case, it would be best either to refer the patient to another therapist, or enter into co-therapy with a therapist trained in bipolar disorder.

83. A: Tell the person that treatment is not always effective. It is unethical to present therapy as always effective for every individual. A therapist should never misrepresent his or her ability or training, or the effectiveness of therapy.

84. A: Explain the purpose of the recording, and obtain the patient's permission, The therapist should inform the patient of the recording, but also gain permission to record. This is also the case when having students involved in treatment or when any other observation by third parties is allowed.

85. C: Facilitate discussion about the patient's options, guiding the patient to review his or her thoughts and feelings about the situation. Ethically, the patient's thoughts and feelings must be respected. It is not the therapist's job to coerce the patient into doing what the therapist feels is best. Each patient must choose for himself or herself.

86. C: Do primarily whatever is in the best interest of the patient. Although it is certainly true that an amicable resolution to the conflict would be beneficial, the primary focus should always be on what is in the best interest of the patient.

87. B: Refer your friend to a therapist you feel would be a good fit. It is not desirable for a therapist to enter into a therapeutic relationship with someone with whom the therapist is personally involved. Such a relationship can make it difficult to maintain objectivity and present an uneven balance of power, among other possible issues.

88. D: Refer your patient to another therapist. Professional conduct and objectivity are critically important in therapy. The therapist must be able to remain objective and keep his or her personal feelings out of the counseling relationship. If the therapist cannot do this, then the patient should be referred to a therapist who can.

89. C: Helping guide the professional in the right thing to do. The code of ethics can help keep a professional out of legal trouble and assist in working with colleagues and legal situations. However, it is primarily a guide in aiding professionals to know the right thing to do.

90. A: Yes. In this situation, the patient is a possible threat to himself or herself and others. In this emergency situation, it would be permissible to restrain the patient. However, unless it is an emergency, a physician's written instructions are required to restrain a patient.

Copyright © Mometrix Media. You have been licensed one copy of this document for personal use only. Any other reproduction or redistribution is strictly prohibited. All rights reserved.

91. B: The thoughts and feelings of the therapist in relation to the patient. At the start of therapy, the patient should be aware of issues regarding time (length, frequency, and duration of sessions), fees, behavioral expectations for both patient and therapist, and the purpose of therapy. The patient does not, however, have the right to know the personal feelings and thoughts of the therapist.

92. C: Yes, if the family member is the patient's legal guardian. If a patient is considered significantly impaired or incompetent, then it is advisable for there to be a legal guardian who is responsible for the patient. In this case, the therapist may discuss the patient's treatment, without written consent from the patient, with the legal guardian.

93. A: Tell him nothing. Confidentiality extends beyond the time that the patient is in treatment. In this example, even though John Smith is no longer in treatment, it is still not permissible to discuss any information about him—even with a family member.

94. C: Discuss her case with him. Confidentiality extends beyond the grave, with the deceased patient's legal representative given the responsibility of providing the release of information after the patient's death. Although laws can vary from state-to-state, it is often permissible to give confidential information to a surviving spouse, who is likely seen as the patient's legal representative after the patient's death.

95. B: Any ages. Substance abuse counselors can work with any population, depending upon their specific training. All ages, including young children and the elderly, can develop substance abuse issues.

96. D: Need ongoing education just like other health professionals. A counselor should ethically maintain the counselor's standard of expertise and stay current within his or her field. What is required to do so will differ from counselor to counselor, but it should be a serious professional consideration.

97. A: Successfully completed your educational training. Some people believe that to be a competent substance abuse counselor, one must have been a substance abuser in the past. This is not true. A past abuser can be a good counselor, but having once abused is not a requirement of competency.

98. C: Work closely with other health disciplines. Because of the nature of substance abuse counseling, counselors often tend to work closely with other health professionals (such as social workers and professionals within the court system).

99. C: Make arrangements depending upon the patients' needs rather than just your own. Whether you are ill or simply going on vacation, the needs of your patients must be kept primary, and the arrangements made for your absence should reflect those concerns.

100. C: Yes, depending upon the circumstances. It is not uncommon for a counselor to be asked to take the place of another counselor during a time of illness or even due to vacation schedules. Whether or not it is appropriate to conduct treatment with another counselor's patient, however, depends upon the needs of the patient and ability of the counselor to meet those needs during the time needed.

Copyright © Mometrix Media. You have been licensed one copy of this document for personal use only. Any other reproduction or redistribution is strictly prohibited. All rights reserved.

Secret Key #1 - Time is Your Greatest Enemy

Pace Yourself

Wear a watch. At the beginning of the test, check the time (or start a chronometer on your watch to count the minutes), and check the time after every few questions to make sure you are "on schedule."

If you are forced to speed up, do it efficiently. Usually one or more answer choices can be eliminated without too much difficulty. Above all, don't panic. Don't speed up and just begin guessing at random choices. By pacing yourself, and continually monitoring your progress against your watch, you will always know exactly how far ahead or behind you are with your available time. If you find that you are one minute behind on the test, don't skip one question without spending any time on it, just to catch back up. Take 15 fewer seconds on the next four questions, and after four questions you'll have caught back up. Once you catch back up, you can continue working each problem at your normal pace.

Furthermore, don't dwell on the problems that you were rushed on. If a problem was taking up too much time and you made a hurried guess, it must be difficult. The difficult questions are the ones you are most likely to miss anyway, so it isn't a big loss. It is better to end with more time than you need than to run out of time.

Lastly, sometimes it is beneficial to slow down if you are constantly getting ahead of time. You are always more likely to catch a careless mistake by working more slowly than quickly, and among very high-scoring test takers (those who are likely to have lots of time left over), careless errors affect the score more than mastery of material.

Secret Key #2 - Guessing is not Guesswork

You probably know that guessing is a good idea - unlike other standardized tests, there is no penalty for getting a wrong answer. Even if you have no idea about a question, you still have a 20-25% chance of getting it right.

Most test takers do not understand the impact that proper guessing can have on their score. Unless you score extremely high, guessing will significantly contribute to your final score.

Monkeys Take the Test

What most test takers don't realize is that to insure that 20-25% chance, you have to guess randomly. If you put 20 monkeys in a room to take this test, assuming they answered once per question and behaved themselves, on average they would get 20-25% of the questions correct. Put 20 test takers in the room, and the average will be much lower among guessed questions. Why?
   1. The test writers intentionally writes deceptive answer choices that "look" right. A

Copyright © Mometrix Media. You have been licensed one copy of this document for personal use only. Any other reproduction or redistribution is strictly prohibited. All rights reserved.

test taker has no idea about a question, so picks the "best looking" answer, which is often wrong. The monkey has no idea what looks good and what doesn't, so will consistently be lucky about 20-25% of the time.

2. Test takers will eliminate answer choices from the guessing pool based on a hunch or intuition. Simple but correct answers often get excluded, leaving a 0% chance of being correct. The monkey has no clue, and often gets lucky with the best choice.

This is why the process of elimination endorsed by most test courses is flawed and detrimental to your performance- test takers don't guess, they make an ignorant stab in the dark that is usually worse than random.

$5 Challenge

Let me introduce one of the most valuable ideas of this course- the $5 challenge:

You only mark your "best guess" if you are willing to bet $5 on it.
You only eliminate choices from guessing if you are willing to bet $5 on it.

Why $5? Five dollars is an amount of money that is small yet not insignificant, and can really add up fast (20 questions could cost you $100). Likewise, each answer choice on one question of the test will have a small impact on your overall score, but it can really add up to a lot of points in the end.

The process of elimination IS valuable. The following shows your chance of guessing it right:

If you eliminate wrong answer choices until only this many remain:	1	2	3
Chance of getting it correct:	100%	50%	33%

However, if you accidentally eliminate the right answer or go on a hunch for an incorrect answer, your chances drop dramatically: to 0%. By guessing among all the answer choices, you are GUARANTEED to have a shot at the right answer.

That's why the $5 test is so valuable- if you give up the advantage and safety of a pure guess, it had better be worth the risk.
What we still haven't covered is how to be sure that whatever guess you make is truly random. Here's the easiest way:

Always pick the first answer choice among those remaining.

Such a technique means that you have decided, **before you see a single test question**, exactly how you are going to guess- and since the order of choices tells you nothing about which one is correct, this guessing technique is perfectly random.

This section is not meant to scare you away from making educated guesses or eliminating choices- you just need to define when a choice is worth eliminating. The $5 test, along with a pre-defined random guessing strategy, is the best way to make sure you reap all of the benefits of guessing.

Copyright © Mometrix Media. You have been licensed one copy of this document for personal use only. Any other reproduction or redistribution is strictly prohibited. All rights reserved.

Secret Key #3 - Practice Smarter, Not Harder

Many test takers delay the test preparation process because they dread the awful amounts of practice time they think necessary to succeed on the test. We have refined an effective method that will take you only a fraction of the time.

There are a number of "obstacles" in your way to succeed. Among these are answering questions, finishing in time, and mastering test-taking strategies. All must be executed on the day of the test at peak performance, or your score will suffer. The test is a mental marathon that has a large impact on your future.

Just like a marathon runner, it is important to work your way up to the full challenge. So first you just worry about questions, and then time, and finally strategy:

Success Strategy

1. Find a good source for practice tests.
2. If you are willing to make a larger time investment, consider using more than one study guide- often the different approaches of multiple authors will help you "get" difficult concepts.
3. Take a practice test with no time constraints, with all study helps "open book." Take your time with questions and focus on applying strategies.
4. Take a practice test with time constraints, with all guides "open book."
5. Take a final practice test with no open material and time limits

If you have time to take more practice tests, just repeat step 5. By gradually exposing yourself to the full rigors of the test environment, you will condition your mind to the stress of test day and maximize your success.

Secret Key #4 - Prepare, Don't Procrastinate

Let me state an obvious fact: if you take the test three times, you will get three different scores. This is due to the way you feel on test day, the level of preparedness you have, and, despite the test writers' claims to the contrary, some tests WILL be easier for you than others.

Since your future depends so much on your score, you should maximize your chances of success. In order to maximize the likelihood of success, you've got to prepare in advance. This means taking practice tests and spending time learning the information and test taking strategies you will need to succeed.

Never take the test as a "practice" test, expecting that you can just take it again if you need to. Feel free to take sample tests on your own, but when you go to take the official test, be prepared, be focused, and do your best the first time!

Copyright © Mometrix Media. You have been licensed one copy of this document for personal use only. Any other reproduction or redistribution is strictly prohibited. All rights reserved.

Secret Key #5 - Test Yourself

Everyone knows that time is money. There is no need to spend too much of your time or too little of your time preparing for the test. You should only spend as much of your precious time preparing as is necessary for you to get the score you need.

Once you have taken a practice test under real conditions of time constraints, then you will know if you are ready for the test or not.
If you have scored extremely high the first time that you take the practice test, then there is not much point in spending countless hours studying. You are already there.

Benchmark your abilities by retaking practice tests and seeing how much you have improved. Once you score high enough to guarantee success, then you are ready.

If you have scored well below where you need, then knuckle down and begin studying in earnest. Check your improvement regularly through the use of practice tests under real conditions. Above all, don't worry, panic, or give up. The key is perseverance!

Then, when you go to take the test, remain confident and remember how well you did on the practice tests. If you can score high enough on a practice test, then you can do the same on the real thing.

Copyright © Mometrix Media. You have been licensed one copy of this document for personal use only. Any other reproduction or redistribution is strictly prohibited. All rights reserved.

General Strategies

The most important thing you can do is to ignore your fears and jump into the test immediately- do not be overwhelmed by any strange-sounding terms. You have to jump into the test like jumping into a pool- all at once is the easiest way.

Make Predictions

As you read and understand the question, try to guess what the answer will be. Remember that several of the answer choices are wrong, and once you begin reading them, your mind will immediately become cluttered with answer choices designed to throw you off. Your mind is typically the most focused immediately after you have read the question and digested its contents. If you can, try to predict what the correct answer will be. You may be surprised at what you can predict.

Quickly scan the choices and see if your prediction is in the listed answer choices. If it is, then you can be quite confident that you have the right answer. It still won't hurt to check the other answer choices, but most of the time, you've got it!

Answer the Question

It may seem obvious to only pick answer choices that answer the question, but the test writers can create some excellent answer choices that are wrong. Don't pick an answer just because it sounds right, or you believe it to be true. It MUST answer the question. Once you've made your selection, always go back and check it against the question and make sure that you didn't misread the question, and the answer choice does answer the question posed.

Benchmark

After you read the first answer choice, decide if you think it sounds correct or not. If it doesn't, move on to the next answer choice. If it does, mentally mark that answer choice. This doesn't mean that you've definitely selected it as your answer choice, it just means that it's the best you've seen thus far. Go ahead and read the next choice. If the next choice is worse than the one you've already selected, keep going to the next answer choice. If the next choice is better than the choice you've already selected, mentally mark the new answer choice as your best guess.

The first answer choice that you select becomes your standard. Every other answer choice must be benchmarked against that standard. That choice is correct until proven otherwise by another answer choice beating it out. Once you've decided that no other answer choice seems as good, do one final check to ensure that your answer choice answers the question posed.

Valid Information

Don't discount any of the information provided in the question. Every piece of information may be necessary to determine the correct answer. None of the information in the question

Copyright © Mometrix Media. You have been licensed one copy of this document for personal use only. Any other reproduction or redistribution is strictly prohibited. All rights reserved.

is there to throw you off (while the answer choices will certainly have information to throw you off). If two seemingly unrelated topics are discussed, don't ignore either. You can be confident there is a relationship, or it wouldn't be included in the question, and you are probably going to have to determine what is that relationship to find the answer.

Avoid "Fact Traps"

Don't get distracted by a choice that is factually true. Your search is for the answer that answers the question. Stay focused and don't fall for an answer that is true but incorrect. Always go back to the question and make sure you're choosing an answer that actually answers the question and is not just a true statement. An answer can be factually correct, but it MUST answer the question asked. Additionally, two answers can both be seemingly correct, so be sure to read all of the answer choices, and make sure that you get the one that BEST answers the question.

Milk the Question

Some of the questions may throw you completely off. They might deal with a subject you have not been exposed to, or one that you haven't reviewed in years. While your lack of knowledge about the subject will be a hindrance, the question itself can give you many clues that will help you find the correct answer. Read the question carefully and look for clues. Watch particularly for adjectives and nouns describing difficult terms or words that you don't recognize. Regardless of if you completely understand a word or not, replacing it with a synonym either provided or one you more familiar with may help you to understand what the questions are asking. Rather than wracking your mind about specific detailed information concerning a difficult term or word, try to use mental substitutes that are easier to understand.

The Trap of Familiarity

Don't just choose a word because you recognize it. On difficult questions, you may not recognize a number of words in the answer choices. The test writers don't put "make-believe" words on the test; so don't think that just because you only recognize all the words in one answer choice means that answer choice must be correct. If you only recognize words in one answer choice, then focus on that one. Is it correct? Try your best to determine if it is correct. If it is, that is great, but if it doesn't, eliminate it. Each word and answer choice you eliminate increases your chances of getting the question correct, even if you then have to guess among the unfamiliar choices.

Eliminate Answers

Eliminate choices as soon as you realize they are wrong. But be careful! Make sure you consider all of the possible answer choices. Just because one appears right, doesn't mean that the next one won't be even better! The test writers will usually put more than one good answer choice for every question, so read all of them. Don't worry if you are stuck between two that seem right. By getting down to just two remaining possible choices, your odds are now 50/50. Rather than wasting too much time, play the odds. You are guessing, but guessing wisely, because you've been able to knock out some of the answer choices that you know are wrong. If you are eliminating choices and realize that the last answer choice you are left with is also obviously wrong, don't panic. Start over and consider each choice again. There may easily be something that you missed the first time and will realize on the second

Copyright © Mometrix Media. You have been licensed one copy of this document for personal use only. Any other reproduction or redistribution is strictly prohibited. All rights reserved.

pass.

Tough Questions

If you are stumped on a problem or it appears too hard or too difficult, don't waste time. Move on! Remember though, if you can quickly check for obviously incorrect answer choices, your chances of guessing correctly are greatly improved. Before you completely give up, at least try to knock out a couple of possible answers. Eliminate what you can and then guess at the remaining answer choices before moving on.

Brainstorm

If you get stuck on a difficult question, spend a few seconds quickly brainstorming. Run through the complete list of possible answer choices. Look at each choice and ask yourself, "Could this answer the question satisfactorily?" Go through each answer choice and consider it independently of the other. By systematically going through all possibilities, you may find something that you would otherwise overlook. Remember that when you get stuck, it's important to try to keep moving.

Read Carefully

Understand the problem. Read the question and answer choices carefully. Don't miss the question because you misread the terms. You have plenty of time to read each question thoroughly and make sure you understand what is being asked. Yet a happy medium must be attained, so don't waste too much time. You must read carefully, but efficiently.

Face Value

When in doubt, use common sense. Always accept the situation in the problem at face value. Don't read too much into it. These problems will not require you to make huge leaps of logic. The test writers aren't trying to throw you off with a cheap trick. If you have to go beyond creativity and make a leap of logic in order to have an answer choice answer the question, then you should look at the other answer choices. Don't overcomplicate the problem by creating theoretical relationships or explanations that will warp time or space. These are normal problems rooted in reality. It's just that the applicable relationship or explanation may not be readily apparent and you have to figure things out. Use your common sense to interpret anything that isn't clear.

Prefixes

If you're having trouble with a word in the question or answer choices, try dissecting it. Take advantage of every clue that the word might include. Prefixes and suffixes can be a huge help. Usually they allow you to determine a basic meaning. Pre- means before, post- means after, pro - is positive, de- is negative. From these prefixes and suffixes, you can get an idea of the general meaning of the word and try to put it into context. Beware though of any traps. Just because con is the opposite of pro, doesn't necessarily mean congress is the opposite of progress!

Hedge Phrases

Watch out for critical "hedge" phrases, such as likely, may, can, will often, sometimes, often, almost, mostly, usually, generally, rarely, sometimes. Question writers insert these hedge

Copyright © Mometrix Media. You have been licensed one copy of this document for personal use only. Any other reproduction or redistribution is strictly prohibited. All rights reserved.

phrases to cover every possibility. Often an answer choice will be wrong simply because it leaves no room for exception. Avoid answer choices that have definitive words like "exactly," and "always".

Switchback Words

Stay alert for "switchbacks". These are the words and phrases frequently used to alert you to shifts in thought. The most common switchback word is "but". Others include although, however, nevertheless, on the other hand, even though, while, in spite of, despite, regardless of.

New Information

Correct answer choices will rarely have completely new information included. Answer choices typically are straightforward reflections of the material asked about and will directly relate to the question. If a new piece of information is included in an answer choice that doesn't even seem to relate to the topic being asked about, then that answer choice is likely incorrect. All of the information needed to answer the question is usually provided for you, and so you should not have to make guesses that are unsupported or choose answer choices that require unknown information that cannot be reasoned on its own.

Time Management

On technical questions, don't get lost on the technical terms. Don't spend too much time on any one question. If you don't know what a term means, then since you don't have a dictionary, odds are you aren't going to get much further. You should immediately recognize terms as whether or not you know them. If you don't, work with the other clues that you have, the other answer choices and terms provided, but don't waste too much time trying to figure out a difficult term.

Contextual Clues

Look for contextual clues. An answer can be right but not correct. The contextual clues will help you find the answer that is most right and is correct. Understand the context in which a phrase or statement is made. This will help you make important distinctions.

Don't Panic

Panicking will not answer any questions for you. Therefore, it isn't helpful. When you first see the question, if your mind goes blank, take a deep breath. Force yourself to mechanically go through the steps of solving the problem and using the strategies you've learned.

Pace Yourself

Don't get clock fever. It's easy to be overwhelmed when you're looking at a page full of questions, your mind is full of random thoughts and feeling confused, and the clock is ticking down faster than you would like. Calm down and maintain the pace that you have set for yourself. As long as you are on track by monitoring your pace, you are guaranteed to have enough time for yourself. When you get to the last few minutes of the test, it may seem like you won't have enough time left, but if you only have as many questions as you should

Copyright © Mometrix Media. You have been licensed one copy of this document for personal use only. Any other reproduction or redistribution is strictly prohibited. All rights reserved.

have left at that point, then you're right on track!

Answer Selection

The best way to pick an answer choice is to eliminate all of those that are wrong, until only one is left and confirm that is the correct answer. Sometimes though, an answer choice may immediately look right. Be careful! Take a second to make sure that the other choices are not equally obvious. Don't make a hasty mistake. There are only two times that you should stop before checking other answers. First is when you are positive that the answer choice you have selected is correct. Second is when time is almost out and you have to make a quick guess!

Check Your Work

Since you will probably not know every term listed and the answer to every question, it is important that you get credit for the ones that you do know. Don't miss any questions through careless mistakes. If at all possible, try to take a second to look back over your answer selection and make sure you've selected the correct answer choice and haven't made a costly careless mistake (such as marking an answer choice that you didn't mean to mark). This quick double check should more than pay for itself in caught mistakes for the time it costs.

Beware of Directly Quoted Answers

Sometimes an answer choice will repeat word for word a portion of the question or reference section. However, beware of such exact duplication – it may be a trap! More than likely, the correct choice will paraphrase or summarize a point, rather than being exactly the same wording.

Slang

Scientific sounding answers are better than slang ones. An answer choice that begins "To compare the outcomes…" is much more likely to be correct than one that begins "Because some people insisted…"

Extreme Statements

Avoid wild answers that throw out highly controversial ideas that are proclaimed as established fact. An answer choice that states the "process should be used in certain situations, if…" is much more likely to be correct than one that states the "process should be discontinued completely." The first is a calm rational statement and doesn't even make a definitive, uncompromising stance, using a hedge word "if" to provide wiggle room, whereas the second choice is a radical idea and far more extreme.

Answer Choice Families

When you have two or more answer choices that are direct opposites or parallels, one of them is usually the correct answer. For instance, if one answer choice states "x increases" and another answer choice states "x decreases" or "y increases," then those two or three answer choices are very similar in construction and fall into the same family of answer choices. A family of answer choices is when two or three answer choices are very similar in

Copyright © Mometrix Media. You have been licensed one copy of this document for personal use only. Any other reproduction or redistribution is strictly prohibited. All rights reserved.

construction, and yet often have a directly opposite meaning.   Usually the correct answer choice will be in that family of answer choices. The "odd man out" or answer choice that doesn't seem to fit the parallel construction of the other answer choices is more likely to be incorrect.

Copyright © Mometrix Media. You have been licensed one copy of this document for personal use only. Any other reproduction or redistribution is strictly prohibited. All rights reserved.

Special Report: Additional Bonus Material

Due to our efforts to try to keep this book to a manageable length, we've created a link that will give you access to all of your additional bonus material.

Please visit http://www.mometrix.com/bonus948/addiction to access the information.

Copyright © Mometrix Media. You have been licensed one copy of this document for personal use only. Any other reproduction or redistribution is strictly prohibited. All rights reserved.

WITHDRAWN

Copyright © Mometrix Media. You have been licensed one copy of this document for personal use only. Any other reproduction or redistribution is strictly prohibited. All rights reserved.